Using Inquiry in the Classroom

Developing Creative Thinkers and Information Literate Students

Second Edition

Teresa Coffman

ROWMAN & LITTLEFIELD EDUCATION

A division of
ROWMAN & LITTLEFIELD PUBLISHERS, INC.
Lanham • New York • Toronto • Plymouth, UK

Published by Rowman & Littlefield Education
A division of Rowman & Littlefield Publishers, Inc.
A wholly owned subsidiary of The Rowman & Littlefield Publishing Group, Inc.
4501 Forbes Boulevard, Suite 200, Lanham, Maryland 20706
www.rowman.com

10 Thornbury Road, Plymouth PL6 7PP, United Kingdom

British Library Cataloguing in Publication Information Available

Library of Congress Cataloging-in-Publication Data

Coffman, Teresa, 1966– author.
  [Engaging students through inquiry-oriented learning and technology]
  Using inquiry in the classroom : developing creative thinkers and information literate
students / Teresa Coffman. — 2nd edition.
      pages cm
  ISBN 978-1-61048-851-8 (cloth : alk. paper) — ISBN 978-1-61048-852-5 (pbk. : alk.
paper) — ISBN 978-1-61048-853-2 (electronic) (print) 1. Inquiry-based learning. 2.
Active learning. 3. Web-based instruction. I. Title.
  LB1027.23.C635 2013
  371.39—dc23   2012034794

∞™ The paper used in this publication meets the minimum requirements of American
National Standard for Information Sciences—Permanence of Paper for Printed Library
Materials, ANSI/NISO Z39.48-1992.

Printed in the United States of America

Contents

Foreword   v

1   What Is Inquiry?   1

2   Designing Instruction for Creative Thinking   19

3   Embedding Information Literacy into Your Course   35

4   Setting Up an Activity: Tying Good Questions to Objectives   49

5   Creating a WebQuest   59

6   Creating a Web Inquiry Activity   83

7   Creating a Telecollaborative Activity   103

8   Creating a Problem-Based Activity   129

9   Inquiry and Creativity in Assessments   139

10   Inquiry in Education Using Technology   153

11   Learning at a Distance   163

References   173

About the Author   179

Foreword

Using Inquiry in the Classroom: Developing Creative Thinkers and Information Literate Students is a must-read for 21st-century educators. Developing creative thinkers and information literate students is important in this knowledge-based economy. Dr. Coffman's book is helpful in identifying effective concepts, strategies, and methods to design a thinking curriculum for students while meeting a teacher's instructional needs.

Throughout the book, instructional strategies and activities are presented that can be integrated into teaching. Coffman provides the reader with transformative ideas that can be seamlessly incorporated into a variety of classroom settings. Any educator whose goal is to develop successful students in this digital age and global environment will want to read this book.

Technology is a reoccurring theme throughout the book, but learning outcomes and meaningful opportunities for students to become engaged in the content and think critically about various topics of instruction are the guiding force and central premise.

As you read and reference Coffman's book, you learn more clearly how to design lessons that allow students to become critical and creative thinkers, and information fluent, and to develop stronger communication and collaboration skills through an authentic learning environment that includes 21st-century resources, tools, and strategies that move you and your students beyond the classroom walls.

This book leads you through an inquiry landscape that provides many opportunities to discover how you can use inquiry-oriented learning strategies and methods in the classroom to help bring your teaching and student learning to life.

You will enjoy this book from cover to cover. Coffman provides effective strategies and methods that you can easily integrate into your own lessons today.

Mary Beth Klinger, Ph.D.
Professor of Business and Economics
College of Southern Maryland

Chapter One

What Is Inquiry?

Welcome to the world of inquiry learning. Defined by experience and exploration, it involves students in the process of learning so they acquire a deeper understanding of the material being taught. Inquiry learning implements a constructivist approach so students interact with the content by asking questions to increase understanding and comprehension and at the same time construct their own knowledge.

The inquiry approach to learning originates in science education, where students create and test a hypothesis (or problem) and throughout the process are encouraged to become actively involved in information discovery by highlighting both the usefulness and application of the information itself. Throughout the process, students discover facts and develop a higher-order understanding of topics and ideas.

Inquiry ensures that students are not only memorizing required factual information, but are also applying the facts to the development of meaningful questions and their own understanding. The questioning approach that is utilized throughout the inquiry process allows students to progress from simply holding and finding factual information to being able to apply new knowledge in novel and different ways.

As a teacher, you can develop inquiry skills in your students by helping them to develop a curiosity of the world around them and then to question and seek answers to help solve relevant problems. This is real-world application of functional skills required to succeed in the world today. And it is very much needed by our 21st-century learners.

OVERVIEW

In the classroom, inquiry-oriented learning can take many forms. Moving away from traditional recitation, the inquiry approach to learning encourages and helps students form their own questions and work through the process of answering them. For example, after studying the Civil War in a history class, the teacher asks students to explore topics that are of unique interest to them.

If a student has a special interest in horses, that student is then encouraged to further explore how horses played an important role in the Civil War: specifically, how generals Robert E. Lee and Stonewall Jackson chose their horses for battle in order to lead their soldiers and missions.

Students learn at a deeper level, in this specific example, about the personalities and characteristics of the two generals and the horses they owned. In so doing, the student learns key information about the Civil War that is of unique interest to himself.

Through inquiry learning, students become actively involved in the inquiry activity by incorporating information literacy skills into solving problems. Skills such as observing, collecting, analyzing, and synthesizing information are developed in order to make predictions and draw conclusions. Inquiry-oriented learning allows students to discover and pursue information with active and engaged involvement in the material.

As the teacher, you can help scaffold and build upon the inquiry process by assisting and encouraging students to ask questions related to the topic being investigated. Each student then has the responsibility to identify and define their own procedures for answering these questions to make the content personal and meaningful to them.

In the Civil War example above, the student no longer sees the two generals as distant historical figures. Through inquiry learning, the Civil War and the two generals now become real and significant. The student digs deeper into the content, asks meaningful questions, and explores the Civil War from a perspective of interest.

MOTIVATION AND INQUIRY

In student learning, motivation is a key element and this is especially critical with inquiry activities. Without student motivation, engagement will not happen and deep inquiry will not take place. When motivated, students are eager to learn, fascinated by their discoveries, and enjoy asking questions.

Motivation is generally either intrinsic or extrinsic. Intrinsic motivation is internal and comes because we are interested in the material and want to do a good job. Extrinsic motivation, on the other hand, comes from external factors, such as good grades or praise on an assignment.

When you begin creating your inquiry activity, try to engage both forms of motivation equally. As shown in Table 1.1, to ensure that each inquiry activity builds on providing both intrinsic and extrinsic motivation, you want the activities to be meaningful, authentic, and challenging, and at the same time align with your learning standards.

In order to create activities that aid in motivating students, you want to make sure that the activity is meaningful and worthwhile. In developing class activities, it is important to ask the following three questions:

1. Why is this important for students to understand?
2. How does this topic relate to their interests?
3. How does this topic tie into their future?

One way to highlight the importance of an activity and motivate your students is to provide connections to their current interests and concerns. For example, in a history class, have students investigate how political elections impact their lives. For an activity, have them prepare and carry out a debate on the impact of voting in society. It is critical to create an activity that connects your students to the content being explored and engages them in the discipline.

Bloom's Taxonomy and Inquiry

Bloom's Taxonomy, originally developed in 1956 and updated in 2000, can help identify and categorize good questions to guide student learning. Within

Table 1.1.   Motivation and Inquiry

Motivation	Examples
Intrinsic	• Authentic activities that are personal, meaningful, challenging, and question your students' existing understanding. • Well-designed activities that encourage curiosity and provide students with some control over their own learning. • Students explore a big idea question about the content that is interesting to them (e.g. How did the Generals of the Civil War choose the horses they did?).
Extrinsic	• Working for good grades and praise for quality work from teachers and classmates. • Thoughtful and reflective comments from the teacher and classmates to aid students and encourage investigation and exploration.

the taxonomy, there are six cognitive levels and these move from lower- to higher-order thinking. The six levels are:

1. Remembering (knowledge)
2. Understanding (comprehension)
3. Applying
4. Analyzing
5. Evaluating
6. Creating (synthesizing)

These six levels provide opportunities for teachers to incorporate inquiry learning into their lessons beyond the lower cognitive-level thinking activities, such as knowledge and comprehension, which center on recitation and memorization, to emphasis on analysis and synthesis.

In order to develop critical thinking and good inquiry activities, you want to ask questions that provide students with opportunities to apply, analyze, synthesize, and evaluate important concepts and themes within the activity. This deeper investigation and exploration of topics allows your students to focus on differentiating and questioning different points of view and then synthesize the information in order to debate an issue or build a model.

At any level within Bloom's Taxonomy, your objective is to identify questions that engage your students and encourage them to ask more in-depth questions about the learning objectives. With Bloom's Taxonomy, it is important that students remember key concepts and understand them, but more importantly, you want them to also begin applying, analyzing, and evaluating these complex ideas.

As you begin to think about creating learning activities within your lesson, you want to identify verbs to help guide you in the design of your questions and activities. See Table 1.2 for an illustration of action verbs that could be used in applying Bloom's Taxonomy to the Civil War example.

By carefully choosing action verbs when designing activities, you will incorporate good questions and guide your students' learning toward higher levels of thought about important topics being explored in your class.

INQUIRY LEARNING

As the teacher, you already use different types of inquiry learning. Historically, teacher-centered learning has been the most popular. Inquiry learning focuses on you asking questions on a consistent basis to ensure that your students understand the material during a class discussion.

Table 1.2. Verbs and Inquiry

Taxonomy	Action Verbs	Question	Activity
Application	Construct	Can you apply the method used to some experience of your own?	Working with a classmate, *construct* a statistical model on the reliability of War strategies used by the Generals.
Analysis	Investigate	What questions would you ask the Generals of the American Civil War knowing what you know now?	Working in small groups, write a letter to both Generals of the Civil War to *investigate* their rationale for going into War.
Synthesis	Proposal	What strategy could President Abraham Lincoln have proposed if he had been able to see into the future for America before the Civil War?	Working with a partner, draft a *proposal* that Abraham Lincoln could have submitted to Congress one month before the Civil War officially started.
Evaluation	Choose	What information is needed in order to defend your position for fighting in the American Civil War?	Working in small groups, create a Web site outlining key strategic moves *chosen* during the Civil War and how these strategies impacted the American people for the duration of the War.

It is also important to get your students actively involved. You ask questions and your students also ask questions by working with their classmates to explore and discover possible answers.

A second type of inquiry learning is student centered. Within this structure of learning, students bring their unique knowledge, understanding, and skills to the learning community. The focus is on the student with an emphasis placed on active engagement in the learning process to develop and build upon student understanding.

Through questioning and discovering information, the student learns the material. The teacher sets up the activity and facilitates the process to ensure students are on task and learning what is intended.

Inquiry follows a process similar to that shown in Figure 1.1. The process begins with questioning and moves through discovery, exploration, and presentation of findings. Throughout this dynamic process, questions are introduced, hypotheses are tested, and new questions are formed and reformed.

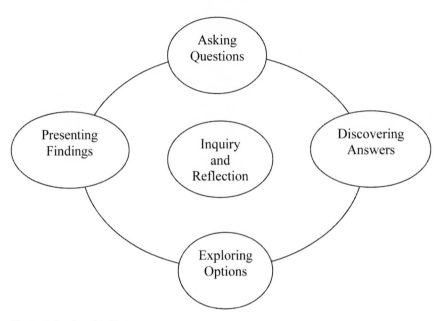

Figure 1.1.   Inquiry Process

Central to this inquiry process is reflection and feedback from the teacher and classmates to ensure that understanding and ultimately learning is occurring.

This is a cyclical process that is in continuous movement between each phase. For this reason, it is necessary to have a project structure in place before inquiry-oriented activities begin. Good planning begins with a clearly identified "big idea" that aligns with the instructional standard.

INQUIRY-ORIENTED LEARNING ACTIVITIES

Inquiry-oriented learning involves any activity that encourages students to think, ask questions, explore information, and then present possible solutions or ideas. This book explores the use of inquiry to encourage creative thinking and support information literacy.

WebQuests, Web inquiry, telecollaborative, and problem-based activities are illustrated as inquiry-oriented learning activities that can be implemented in the classroom to engage students in the learning process. Each activity is similar because each uses the Internet to discover and explore as well as share information. A discussion on assessments and a concluding chapter in learning at a distance are also provided.

By incorporating WebQuests, Web inquiry, telecollaborative, and problem-based activities into your classroom, students have a variety of opportunities to construct their own understanding of topics as they are explored in class. Through the process of inquiry, your students will be engaged, motivated, and eager to learn new ideas and concepts.

The inquiry process involves:

- Identifying questions to find possible answers;
- Identifying appropriate and quality resources to aid students in answering the identified questions;
- Manipulating resources to ensure that correct information is identified and answers to specific questions are explored; and
- Formulating answers discovered and identifying how these answers relate back to the original questions.

Your role as the teacher in the inquiry process is to create meaningful activities that engage your students and capture their attention so they are motivated to learn and discover information by asking questions and then sharing that new knowledge with others in meaningful ways. Below is a short summary of each technology-related inquiry activity to be discussed in the text.

WebQuests

A WebQuest is an inquiry-oriented activity that primarily uses the Internet for resources. WebQuests are generally developed around a theme. For example, students create a newspaper that highlights the times of Christopher Columbus and the story of Columbus, particularly his quest for India. The newspaper can also compare and contrast Columbus's experiences to other explorers past and present.

WebQuests can be completed individually or in small groups. If done in a group setting, students can role-play different characters or be assigned different topics within the overall theme, such as in the example of the newspaper. Students are assigned roles such as the queen, Columbus, ship reporters, and natives, and then gather and report on their specific role during that time period.

This diverse learning experience provides students with opportunities to learn about and tell the individual stories of each role and then share their findings in the format of a newspaper that can then be published either on the Internet or in the school newspaper to be shared with others.

In a WebQuest, students are provided with questions and resources that they use in order to discover and explore information. Students then present their findings. Figure 1.2 provides an example of a quest and inquiry.

Out at Sea WebQuest

You are in charge of the ship's "Journey Journal." The journal contains many different items. You need to complete all the tasks and put the information together in a Journey Journal notebook.

Step One: Biographical Information on the Explorer

In order to do a good job for your Captain, you must understand who he or she is. Let's start by first watching a short video about explorers in general. *Watch the video.*

Now that you know more about explorers of the world, it is time to concentrate on your explorer. Click on the *Explorer Worksheet* and answer all the questions about your assigned explorer. Next, you will share your findings about your explorer with the class, so make sure you print out your report and place it in your "Journey Journal."

Step Two: Cargo and Food Report

As you set sail for the exploration, you must make sure that your ship's cargo list is complete.

Ensure that the ship is fully stocked with food for your crew for the long voyage. Gather information about foods that were available during the time period of your explorer and design a list of items you will need for your ship. Make sure you address such questions as:

> What will the crew drink?
> Will you stop along the way to get more food?
> Will you fish or hunt for food?

What else will you bring on your voyage? Investigate what else your explorer might have brought with him or her by thinking about what kind of clothes were needed, types of tools needed, trading trinkets, or any other items you discover.

When you have your ship's Cargo and Food Report completed, add it to your "Journey Journal."

Step Three: Navigator Report

Now that your ship is fully stocked, it is time to set sail. But how will the Captain know where to go? Well, as his or her first mate it is your job to make sure the Captain has the appropriate maps and directions to reach the destination.

First, determine how explorers navigated their ships during this time period and report your findings so that the Captain can have those instruments on the ship when it sets sail.

Second, create a map of the journey the explorer took to reach his or her destination. Print out a world map that shows where your explorer began and the

Figure 1.2.   WebQuest and Inquiry

route taken to reach the final destination. Make sure you label your map with the following information (A map Web site is available for your use):

- Country that the ship started its voyage in.
- Country where the ship ended its voyage.
- The body of water the ship traveled across.
- The Equator and the different hemispheres.
- Draw a navigational symbol showing North, South, East, and West.

Also, draw a picture of the ship and what it must have looked like when it landed at its destination. Don't forget to take note of such things as wildlife or rivers in your drawing.

Add all these items to your "Journey Journal."

Step Four: Achievements of Explorer Report

LAND AHeeeeeaaaad......

You have safely made it to your destination!

Now as the first mate, it is your responsibility to act as the reporter to report back to the homeland new discoveries such as:

- Where did you land?
- What did you find?
- Where there any native people there?
- Who are they and what are they like?
- Are there raw materials to build homes or survive? What kind of homes might you build?
- Are there plants to eat or should seed be sent over on future voyages?
- What kind of wildlife is there?
- Is this the final destination of the Explorer or does he or she set sail soon afterwards and explore further?

The King and Queen are very curious people so your report must be detailed. Your report should be about two pages in length. It should tell of your adventure and the discovery of this new land and what it has to offer. Don't forget to include in your report at least two drawings of your findings so that they can see what this new land looks like.

Add all these items to your "Journey Journal."

WebQuests can be completed in varying lengths of time, from one to two class periods to an entire unit of instruction. Activities include collecting and then sharing information. The information can be disseminated and shared through preparation for a debate or presentation, writing an editorial to be published in the local paper, or presenting at the next parent conference or community meeting.

As its name implies, this is a quest. Therefore, it should be fun, informative, and exciting, and engaging, while at the same time inquiry based.

Web Inquiry

Web-inquiry activities are not as involved or in-depth as WebQuests. Web-inquiry activities look at raw data. From these data, students explore and make predictions based on their analysis. The teacher is responsible for identifying the questions and the students are responsible for identifying the specific procedures and strategies for obtaining the appropriate information for the questions posed.

Web inquiry is a form of guided inquiry and therefore it is important to provide appropriate resources to aid students in answering content questions. At the same time, students should also be encouraged to find additional resources to help answer the questions posed.

Through Web inquiry, students learn how to manipulate and explore raw data with the resources provided by the teacher. They are then guided toward finding the information requested through structured scaffolding.

For example, a student studying economics could be directed by the teacher to the U.S. Department of Labor's Bureau of Labor Statistics Web site at http://www.bls.gov/ to find actual data on labor in the local area and statistics related to the economy. This is the "real" data that U.S. government economists refer to and use to create meaning around many important decisions regarding the U.S. economy.

Telecollaborative

Telecollaborative activities are another form of inquiry-oriented learning that additionally involves students collecting and sharing data. The main difference with this activity as opposed to WebQuests or Web inquiry projects is that during a telecollaborative activity, students collect and share data with other students, outside experts, and other teachers in different locations (outside the classroom) using Internet collaboration and communication tools.

Students have the ability to work collaboratively with you and other students, as well as experts around the world, to solve workable and at times complex problems. This inquiry-oriented activity links your students and resources together so they can identify key questions from data collected around the globe. The key idea is working collaboratively using the Internet with individuals outside of the classroom.

For example, students in a science class participate in a global experiment to determine how much water they use every day and then compare that to how much water communities around the world use each day at CIESE, The

Center for Innovation in Engineering and Science Education, at http://www .ciese.org/collabprojs.html.

Through inquiry-based questioning, data collection, and conversations with experts in the field, students start to think about water usage around the world. This exercise gets students engaged and excited about learning.

Problem Based

Problem-based activities are a dynamic way for students to explore real-world problems and challenges. Student learning takes place in a specific learning situation and is dependent on the environment. Because problem-based learning is situational, it can take many different forms.

The objective is to develop student research and collaboration skills, as well as improve creative thinking, by having students ask good questions and be actively engaged with the content. Cognitive engagement is the central goal of a problem-based learning activity.

Developing a problem-based learning activity first requires a good understanding of the problem and the situation, as well as how the project best fits into your overall curriculum content. From there, students should have enough time to research the problem, review one another's work, and provide constructive feedback—all the while using technology tools seamlessly throughout the activity.

Problem-based activities can assist students in becoming independent learners who are capable of developing higher-order thinking skills.

In the chapters that follow WebQuests, Web inquiry, telecollaborative, and problem-based activities will be explored in-depth so that you can learn to develop and utilize these inquiry tools in your own classroom to support and enhance inquiry-oriented learning. Inquiry-oriented learning is an important and effective way to teach and learn. Not only will you enjoy this student-centered approach, but so too will your students.

Inquiry-oriented learning is also an exciting way to share knowledge that exists outside the classroom. It also provides opportunities for encouraging 21st-century skills needed by all students in today's world.

Using an inquiry-oriented learning approach allows students to:

- Explore and discover content through an authentic and challenging learning context;
- Create and test a hypothesis through authentic and real-world tools;
- Learn and explore content within a collaborative environment;
- Gain self-efficacy with prior knowledge and expand new knowledge; and
- Use technology to enhance and strengthen higher-order thinking.

PROMOTING AND APPLYING
INQUIRY IN YOUR CLASSROOM

To promote inquiry in the classroom, you want to first identify a "big idea" in the content being explored. The "big idea" is an overarching question that guides instruction, emphasizes the main idea of the unit, and is connected to the learning standards. Once the "big idea" question is identified, encourage students to identify sub-questions, plan and conduct investigations, and work in small groups to identify solutions or possible answers to the questions posed.

For example, in a unit that teaches sixth graders about economics, specifically a learning standard that looks at the relationship between money and different societies throughout the world, a "big idea" question might be: *How have money and other means of commerce taken shape throughout history and across different civilizations?*

As a class, the teacher leads a brainstorming session by posing this "big idea" question and then guides students to think about how money and bartering have changed throughout societies. As students are brainstorming, the teacher scribes their ideas on an interactive white board.

Once students finish suggesting ideas, they can organize the collection of ideas into categories. Once the categories are organized, students can brainstorm possible sub-questions for each category. Once the sub-questions are identified, as a collective group the class can then decide which questions and categories they want to work on and understand better.

In small groups or as a class, students can then begin their inquiry. The notes of this brainstorming session can be saved and posted to the class Web site so everyone has a reference point to stay connected to the overall goal of the activity. Figure 1.3 outlines the questioning process.

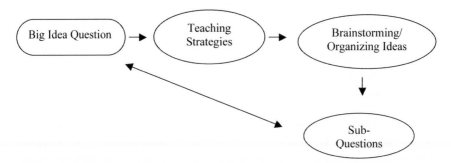

Figure 1.3.   Questioning Process

As this example illustrates, throughout the inquiry process your students are involved in their own learning. This is true for all inquiry projects. Inquiry learning allows students to develop strategies and methods for deep investigation and exploration into important topics explored in class as they relate to the student.

Through this process, you are teaching your students how to ask questions and how to be involved in their learning process. Inquiry-oriented learning is not passive; rather, it is an active and engaged process that leads to higher-order thinking.

Throughout the inquiry process, students work in collective groups and as a class to identify what they already know about a given topic as well as what they do not know. As the teacher, you encourage students to identify key points of interest about the topic. You also support them as they begin asking deeper questions to explore their interests further as they relate to the intended learning objective for the lesson.

Through this process of collaboration and investigation, students begin to understand the "big idea" of the lesson and the larger picture, e.g., their personal world. Inquiry learning is beginning to take shape.

TAKING CARE OF YOUR STUDENTS

Although student centered, your students need guidance when working with inquiry activities. As the teacher, you want to ensure that students receive guidance in the activity as well as have plenty of opportunities for practice and feedback.

Traditionally, teaching has focused on dispensing knowledge and information to students through lecture, memorization, and skill-specific tasks. Once the student completes a specific task, they complete a paper, a presentation, and/or an objective test.

In an inquiry assignment, the teacher provides students with an open-ended question, e.g., the "big idea" question. From there, students are encouraged to ask further questions and are provided good resources and tools.

Students are often placed into small homogeneous groups so they can conduct research, ask questions, and ultimately present their findings in meaningful ways such as a debate, an editorial for the school paper, or a letter to a community leader to share information on a political or social topic.

Through this inquiry process, you eventually want your students to take the lead in asking questions, investigating good resources, and identifying solutions. However, to fully focus and engage them in the learning process, each activity must begin with a "big idea" question. This question must capture your students' attention and encourage them to ask follow-up questions, make predictions, and discover new information.

A "big idea" question such as: *What happens if an animal or plant is removed from the food web?* allows students to creatively explore this science concept from a broad perspective and to think more critically about food webs in general.

Ultimately, it allows students to see how this web impacts life as a whole. Additional layers to this question can be added to the original "big idea" question as students develop explanations, evaluate predictions, and further expand their understanding.

Now you try it. Use table 1.3 below to formulate a "big idea" question and then relate it back to your course content standards and learning objectives. Prepare two "big idea" questions that you want your students to investigate and explore, identify which content standards your questions align with, and then list objectives that are met with these two inquiry explorations.

In this approach, students are encouraged to:

- Become self-directed learners intrinsically motivated through their discoveries;
- Work collaboratively with classmates through cooperative learning strategies and methods;
- Become actively engaged in the learning activity and task at hand;
- Share new knowledge through a presentation or performance; and
- Develop higher-order thinking skills.

Table 1.3. Big Idea Questions

Big Idea Question	Content Standards	Learning Objectives
1)		
2)		

CREATIVITY AND INQUIRY

Inquiry-oriented learning is a creative form of learning in which students take an active role and are guided by you, the teacher. You need to provide questions about course objectives as well as provide resources to provide a rich learning environment where your students are actively engaged in critical thinking and creativity. Through inquiry the focus is on the big picture of the learning unit, e.g., why is this important to me?

Throughout this process you should:

- Create an authentic and meaningful task. This task must be wrapped around the most important concepts from your activity or unit that you want your students to know;
- Implement continued and authentic assessments that include real-world tasks that demonstrate understanding and knowledge creation;
- Identify the educational goals of the lesson along with appropriate objectives;
- Facilitate inquiry throughout the learning process to guide students in higher-order thinking by having students question and reflect on their findings; and
- Be comfortable learning along with your students.

21ST-CENTURY SKILLS

As you develop and identify the "big idea" for your unit and learning objective, you should also think about how to integrate 21st-century skills into your learning unit. Planning for inquiry projects goes beyond having students achieve content knowledge. Planning should also engage students into practicing higher-order thinking skills such as applying, analyzing, synthesizing, and evaluating information in order to create a new understanding of knowledge.

Inquiry-oriented activities have the potential to provide students with opportunities to develop these necessary skills by encouraging them to work on problems and identify questions to determine possible solutions. The idea is for you to ask questions that your students are concerned about and then to tie these questions into course standards.

When educators talk about 21st-century skills and preparing students for the world outside of a school's traditional four walls, the emphasis is on developing creative thinkers and self-directed risk takers who are able to ask thoughtful questions.

With inquiry-oriented learning, the classroom becomes an open and collaborative environment where students work in small and large groups inside and outside the classroom to help develop skills that will enable them to be successful in the world.

Through carefully planned activities, students are taught how to prioritize investigations and discoveries by working closely with team members and the teacher. Students have opportunities to solve problems using some of the same tools that experts in the field use.

For example, if students are creating a food web habitat in a science course, small groups are formed to look for evidence of specific impact on ecosystems and habitats when a plant or an animal has changed in that habitat. Each small group works on a food web, identifying their hypotheses as to what changes in the habitat if the web is altered.

Then groups look for evidence using online databases to collect real data to support their specific hypotheses. This type of active and engaged learning stimulates and excites students and ultimately promotes new knowledge.

Information Technology and Inquiry Learning

Inquiry learning lessons focus on the "big idea" as identified by the teacher. It is from this big idea that your students create a hypothesis. The central focus is for students to begin asking relevant questions and begin the process of research and discovery. Using the food web example, the teacher could show a video and have a discussion, or create a wiki to work collaboratively and then share new knowledge with others outside of the class.

Students could also keep a reflection journal of their new knowledge on a class blog that could be shared with other classes and parents all around elements of a food web and the importance of its interrelationships. Next, the class could talk about how scientists use analogies and comparisons to make predictions and then develop theories.

Technology provides an effective and engaging way for students to become investigators of knowledge and to help them create new understanding of course topics. The power of technology tools is that they allow students to communicate with their teachers, classmates, and other students, as well as experts outside the classroom in a global context.

Technology tools, such as the Internet and software programs, such as presentation software, allow student-collected data to be stored and shared and then presented in new and meaningful ways.

Technology tools allow opportunities for students to:

• Create mental images through concept maps and electronic journals;
• Explore databases with raw data and primary source documents, images, and films;

- Communicate with other classmates in the classroom or the school, as well as with students in other locations around the country or world; and
- Ask experts in the field of study where students are investigating to get a real-world perspective on an issue or concept.

Most importantly, technology tools provide opportunities for students to investigate and explore the world just as professionals do out in the field. This real-world learning and application is exactly what the inquiry-oriented approach to learning is all about.

CHAPTER SUMMARY

In this chapter, key elements found in inquiry-oriented activities were identified. The primary goal in inquiry learning is to pose a question that relates to the standards of learning as well as student interests. Questions should be broad and at the same time answerable.

Activities should provide students with opportunities to create hypotheses and then test their hypotheses in small homogeneous groups. Throughout an activity, students should have ample opportunity to reflect on their understanding and share this new knowledge with their classmates. By the end of an activity, students have a product that can be shared with others.

In the chapters that follow, we will explore creative thinking, demonstrate how to embed information literacy into your course, and then look at objectives and how teachers can align standards to inquiry-oriented questions.

CHAPTER REFLECTION

1. How can you integrate inquiry-oriented teaching and learning into the way you presently teach?
2. What does it mean to incorporate a "big idea" question into your classroom project? List a "big idea" question for a unit you are planning to teach within the next month.
3. Identify teaching and learning strategies you can use to engage your students in exploring your "big idea" question.

Chapter Two

Designing Instruction for Creative Thinking

Creativity is everywhere. And it is an essential component of an effective curriculum. Today's learners must be creatively focused, engaged, and motivated as well as excited to see what lies ahead in their journey. This second chapter explores the multifaceted world of creativity from an instructional standpoint.

You will emerge from this chapter with a better understanding of the difference between "inquiry" versus "creative" thinking, appreciate how theory impacts the overall teaching practice, build skills to encourage your students to see learning in a different light, and gain a stronger understanding of a "thinking curriculum."

OVERVIEW

Introducing creative thinking into the process of learning can be a difficult task, but it is one that you are ready for. The main premise of creative thinking is to help your students become innovative and inventive thinkers. When you incorporate technology tools into this approach, you have the potential to further engage students into the world of inquiry learning.

As you incorporate creative or divergent thinking into your instruction, think beyond the creative arts. At their core, creative arts involves creativity, but when developing a creative-thinking approach, we want to incorporate inventive thinking as well. All students should be encouraged to think entrepreneurially as well as creatively.

Consider strategies and approaches that help your students go beyond the obvious and encourage them to generate and extend ideas, suggest and explore hypotheses, and apply their own imagination to the process. Each of these can help students determine alternatives to a proposed problem that they encounter in your classroom or elsewhere.

For example, suppose that your next lesson is on weather patterns. You introduce weather by designing an inquiry-oriented lesson that incorporates creative thinking. First, you identify some good questions to get your students thinking about weather more broadly than they have in the past.

You design an activity using real-weather data from the National Oceanic and Atmospheric Administration (NOAA) in Washington, D.C. NOAA collects real-time data and stores them in a database so that scientists, teachers, and researchers from around the world can access the information to make discoveries about weather patterns and tendencies throughout the years.

For the activity, you identify an essential question for your students to explore about weather. Your "big idea" question is: *How does climate change impact your daily life?*

In class, you start by asking students this "big idea" question. From there, you pull up the U.S. climate map at http://www.ncdc.noaa.gov/oa/climate/research/cag3/cag3.html and explore it as a class. With the "big idea" question in each student's mind, they then begin thinking about how to answer the question by looking at the data before them.

As the activity develops, your questioning can also advance. Ultimately, you are encouraging students to begin thinking creatively about this issue in inventive and imaginative ways.

By asking "what" and "what if" questions, you can usually get students more involved and motivated. For example, to get students thinking about what they have experienced over a particular season, ask them the following question: *What type of weather have we experienced so far this winter?*

After they share their experiences, go back to the U.S. climate map and draw their attention to the primary source data on the climate map. Students examine the data and information and go on and make informed decisions and predictions for the rest of the season or possibly even for the next winter season.

While looking at the map, ask students to identify on the climate map any similarities of what they experienced this past winter and what is displayed on the map. Is it accurate in their view? What is missing? What additional information is needed?

By using technology in this way, e.g., displaying real-world data and involving your students in a discussion around higher-order tasks, you are helping them connect to their learning. In essence, they are using information in multiple ways.

This allows students to build on their personal experience and gain new knowledge. You are also illustrating to students that collected and established data have value and allow them to make inferences about the world around them for current and future use.

As the activity progresses, continue to provide your students with scaffolding experiences. Give them opportunities to think about their learning and the content in a different and more personal way. The data that you identified as important can now be used by your students to identify weather patterns and to make inferences about weather in their environment and around their neighborhood.

Up to this point, you have been asking students to think about their experiences with the weather and then relate them to actual recorded data. Next, you want to build a more extensive questioning technique so that students can develop a deeper understanding about the topic.

To dig deeper into building connections, encourage your students (not you) to ask questions about the data. For example, start off by asking them: *What types of patterns are visible when looking at winter weather in your geographic area over the past five years?*

Organize their thinking around your original essential question on weather patterns and climate change, e.g., *How does climate change impact your daily life?* As a class, pull up the data from the past five years for each winter month from the climate map. Have students break into small groups to investigate the data and analyze the information presented. Ask each group to predict next winter after determining the pattern over the past five years.

Throughout this process, your role is to help garner creative thinking and ideas. You want to encourage students to build their own questions around what they see on the climate map and the world around them. During this time, you also are talking the language of weather and so are your students. You highlight terms such as longitude and latitude, jet stream, ocean currents, and land mass, to name a few.

As your students begin using the proper language and critically examine the climate map, they are able to seek out patterns and make predictions. They are building on their personal multidimensional thinking by altering and developing deeper understanding.

When you make your activities personal and use technology as a real-world tool, your lessons become more meaningful. When you build creative-thinking activities into your lessons, through questioning and discovery, you help students think about the content and their world differently.

You are also helping them to build the necessary skills to answer new and future-oriented questions. Many of these answers and ideas we do not even know the questions to yet. This is our 21st-century learner.

So, let's continue to make this personal to students by posing a scientific problem that you just heard about on the local news while driving into work.

Gardeners and horticulturalists are finding that plant species are blooming earlier than normal and they are concerned that this may have a direct impact on pollination. You tell your students about this concern in class that day and encourage their interest by identifying an experiment they can be involved in.

You introduce the project, Project Budburst, telling students that they will all be scientists, collecting data in their neighborhoods. Students are reminded that the class is still in the process of answering the original question, e.g., *How does climate change impact your daily life?* To extend this question further, the class will now look at how weather has impacted pollination in the neighborhood.

Students begin by collecting data on plant species that bloom in their neighborhood. They sketch or take pictures of the species, identify the species, and keep a science journal, identifying the date, time, and a brief note of their specimens. Each student then analyzes their personal data by doing deeper research to determine the average bloom dates for their specimens.

Data can come from your local agricultural extension agent or the extension agency's Web site or from library resources within your school. Make sure to talk with your librarian before your project so you can set up data sources for your students to obtain information from.

Once students collect their necessary data from their personal investigation and further research, it is time to begin comparing the average bloom times with the actual bloom times with the winter climate data identified. Ask your students to think about the U.S. climate map and the insights they gained from this activity.

Next, ask about patterns they see emerging from the bloom data they found. After your discussion, have students enter their data into the Project Budburst database, http://neoninc.org/budburst/, a science initiative that tracks the timing of flowering plants across the country. Now your students work has just become even more real by adding to the data that can be used by others in their search to discover patterns in weather data.

So far, your students have participated in their own learning by looking at primary data, collecting their own primary data, and ultimately being asked to think about weather and their community in new ways.

Accordingly, the creative thinking and design comes about in the following manner:

• Through questioning and engaging students in the process of their own learning;
• By exploring topics and content with primary data; and
• By thinking about it in new ways to make informed discoveries and decisions.

As you think about activities that involve creative thinking, put on your own creative-thinking hat. You also need to be a creative thinker to effectively integrate creative-thinking activities and lessons into your curriculum. New knowledge discovery occurs by asking higher-level questions, using real data to make informed decisions, and most importantly going beyond the obvious answer to identify your own personal hypotheses.

The entire activity outlined above is both messy and focused. Having your students think about weather by making it personal and designing the lesson through asking and answering tough unpredictable questions will help students develop and build necessary skills.

These skills are necessary in order to work with ambiguity and ultimately cultivate complex thinking. The skills learned in this context can be taken with them to higher grades and will eventually lend themselves well to life's experiences.

CREATIVE-THINKING PRINCIPLES

As you integrate creative thinking into your curriculum, begin to consider specific principles or strategies of thinking that can be integrated into your lessons. The goal is to help your students develop multiple ways of knowing, such as a sense of reason, logic, resourcefulness, imagination, and innovation.

In thinking about the design of your lesson to incorporate these creative-thinking principles, consider the most appropriate sequencing and scaffolding of your lesson to build a solid knowledge base for your students. In so doing, they will develop a sophisticated understanding of your topic that will then help build on their knowledge to broader ideas and more sophisticated concepts.

For example, let's say you are teaching your students about three-dimensional figures and volume. Your objective is for students to use formulas for surface area and volume of three-dimensional objects to solve real-world problems. You incorporate Google Earth at http://www.google.com/earth into your activity to help students understand this concept.

You also search the Web site Real World Math at http://www.realworld math.org/ and find a lesson plan that you can tailor to meet your specific student needs and your Standards of Learning (SOLs). Your goal is to sequence the instruction to help students develop sophisticated thinking patterns around volume and three dimensions.

As you pull up Google Earth on the classroom computer, you identify the goal of the day's activity: *To find the volume and the surface area in a 3D environment using an appropriate formula.*

You load the Geometric Solids .Kmz file into Google Earth that you found located in the Real World Math Web site and retrieve the *Pyramids of Egypt* to display on the class computer. You pan around the pyramids and ask your students questions about what they see.

During this question-and-answer session, you incorporate terms and concepts that are important for students to understand and relate to the world around them. You scaffold your questions, helping your students see the different dimensions of the triangle shapes and encouraging them to think about the ratios of length, perimeter, area, and volume. At each stage, students concentrate on the changes in volume and question what that means mathematically.

Throughout the lesson, you are building and developing students' mathematical-thinking strategies. With each lesson, they become more confident and mathematically literate. As you develop your activity, the students can branch out to find new triangle shapes in the world around them and practice what they learned. Thus, you are teaching your students to be enterprising and adaptable.

As students improve their understanding of volume and surface area, you are also helping them develop confidence and purpose in their own learning. They are able to generate and apply new ideas and concepts that they are experiencing through the activity in a specific context, but at the same time, they are also discovering how to learn and gain new knowledge in innovative ways.

As you combine and build on the main idea of your math lesson on volume and area, students are introduced to new possibilities to refine their prior knowledge and build upon their own personal theories through the development of their own understanding.

This is necessary for creative thinking to be successful. As learners, students must continually question the world around them. Your role is to help facilitate this development by asking scaffolding questions and allowing students to utilize critical-thinking skills, such as interpreting, analyzing, evaluating, explaining, sequencing, reasoning, comparing, questioning, inferring, hypothesizing, appraising, testing, and generalizing throughout the process.

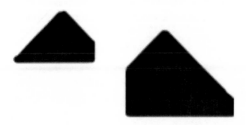

Figure 2.1. Volume and Surface Area

ORGANIZING ELEMENTS OF THINKING

Let's organize the critical- and creative-thinking learning continuum into interconnected parts. Each part of this whole will provide a different and dynamic aspect of thinking for your students. When thinking about each of these parts, do not think of them as a taxonomy of thinking. Rather, they serve as a cohesive whole that needs to be simultaneously developed throughout the learning process.

In a creative-thinking activity, your goal is to have students think broadly and deeply using skills, behaviors, and dispositions that they will need for a lifetime. Some of these dispositions include the ability to reason, identify logic, be resourceful, use their imagination, and be original.

In order to do this, your students must be able to generate and evaluate knowledge, clarify concepts and ideas, and seek possibilities that may not be obvious. While at the same time, they should be considering alternatives to solve complex problems, even if others have not yet thought of these alternatives.

Our 21st-century students need to be entrepreneurial and use their imagination to identify new possibilities. Thus, when examining the climate map and then collecting data, students not only record data, but also analyze its impact on their own personal environment as well as the larger world. This moves students away from the singular textbook and opens up the learning process to become more personal and meaningful.

A STANDARDS-BASED CURRICULUM

These ideas continue to be important in a standards-based curriculum. Students build on the facts that they have learned and develop higher abilities to

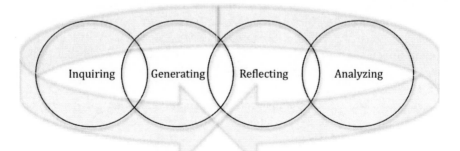

Figure 2.2.   Creative Thinking Continuum

build new knowledge around more complex topics that they will explore next in their classroom or in an advanced grade level.

To illustrate another example, suppose that in a literature class you decide to incorporate critical-thinking skills into your next lesson. You want students to read and analyze relationships among American literature, history, and culture. Specifically, you want students to recognize how authors are influenced by the ideas and values of their times.

The book chosen for the lesson, *To Kill a Mockingbird*, centers around a Southern town that is confronting its own prejudices regarding race. As students read the story, you point out key ideas, e.g., that this is a coming-of-age memoir from the perspective of a young Southern girl growing up during the Great Depression of the 1930s.

The takeaway is that you want your students to develop an ability to see situations in new ways and begin to develop connections and similarities between literature and real life. In this example, students start developing a process of exploring their own creative thinking around language and literature.

In a class discussion, you direct students to identify themes presented throughout the book. One such theme is the existence of social inequality and prejudice. As students discuss this theme, guide them to questions of prejudice and our need as a society to work to resolve this issue.

Students should be able to relate to issues of discrimination and discuss examples of people being denied their rights as a result of prejudice. Bringing the conversation back to the book, you mention Tom Robinson and other African Americans in the novel. Then, you ask students to think about experiences they encountered in today's world that relate to prejudice.

As the discussion ensues, you bring up the Merriam-Webster Online Dictionary Web site on the class computer at http://www.merriam-webster.com/, and type "prejudice" in the search engine. A definition displays in the front of the classroom. You have students read the definition. You do the same for the word "discrimination."

Students can then be placed in small groups and create their own definitions of prejudice and discrimination. Ask them to share their definitions with the larger group. Working with partners, have students record two specific examples of prejudice from the novel by providing specific incidences, who was involved, at what point in the novel's plot the examples occurred, and what the effect of this incident had on the characters and the plot itself.

Once completed, have students combine their findings in a class chart that is displayed on the classroom computer. This can be a Google document, http://docs.google.com/, that enables the information to be collected and shared with the group. Once the chart is populated, have students share their findings with the class.

To bring this activity back to the learning goal of relating to society, have students depict racial prejudice and discrimination throughout history. Students can take a virtual field trip at the interactive tour of the Civil Rights Museum, http://www.civilrightsmuseum.org/, and identify the beginnings of the civil rights movement, one important leader of this movement, when the person was born, and his or her most important contribution(s).

From there, students can explain at least one successful action organized and carried out by the civil rights movement to achieve fair treatment for African Americans, identifying key people involved, when the incident took place, and the overall effect. These findings can be shared with the class.

Students can also work in small groups to create a presentation using a technology tool, such as VoiceThread, http://voicethread.com/, to highlight what they learned about the themes of prejudice and discrimination in the novel and how these ideas related to the civil rights movement.

Have students personalize these ideas by thinking about their own experiences with these themes and a current issue relating to prejudice and discrimination in the media. Have students describe the impact of their example on themselves and among their peers.

Themes in novels are just as important today as they were when they were written, such as in the 1960s book *To Kill a Mockingbird*. Your goal is to help students build thinking skills to critically explore texts and begin justifying a point of view. This is a personal point of view encapsulated with the views of others.

Through reading and questioning, students explore assumptions made and begin to question those assumptions. This exercise teaches students to respond to others' views with good information and inquiry.

Mathematics is no different than literature in terms of inquiry learning and creative thinking. Lesson-specific strategies can be designed for students to generate and evaluate knowledge, clarify concepts and ideas, and seek possibilities and alternatives as they solve mathematical problems. This mathematical thinking is a core standard of a successful mathematics curriculum where students think about how to solve problems and decipher methods and strategies so they can determine a workable solution.

Some ways this can be accomplished within a lesson is to have students justify their choice in an equation or calculation strategy used. You can also have them identify relevant questions that can be asked during a statistical investigation. Encourage your students to look for alternative ways to approach a problem, such as identifying when a problem is similar to the previous one, drawing diagrams, or simplifying a problem to control variables.

In science, creating and creative thinking are embedded into skills of questioning, making predictions, speculating, solving problems through investigation, making evidence-based decisions, and analyzing and evaluating evidence. Your students develop each of these thinking skills by active inquiry that involves planning, selecting appropriate information, and evaluating sources of information—all to formulate conclusions.

Scientific thinking is conducive to creative thinking because it promotes flexibility and open-mindedness, allowing students to speculate about their observations of the world, and from those observations begin developing a conceptual framework that becomes increasingly more sophisticated as they actively acquire more information.

In history, creative thinking allows students to question sources, interpret the past from incomplete documentation, develop arguments using evidence, and assess reliability when they select and use information from resources. Creative thinking allows students to develop new interpretations from these old ideas to explain aspects of the past that are either contested or now well understood.

THEORETICAL UNDERPINNINGS

Many educational researchers have categorized critical and creative thinking as dispositions, taxonomies of skills, frames of mind, thinking strategies, and even philosophical inquiry. Within each of these ideas, a capability is believed to be developed that allows students to acquire a skill or behavior such as learning.

As a teacher, your goal with creative thinking is to help develop adventurous thinkers: thinkers that are strategic, metacognitive, and most importantly will persevere by taking risks when they are confronted with continuous problems where there is no easy solution.

Gardner (2009) and later Robinson (2010) emphasized that each of us have natural abilities and talents as learners. These abilities can come in many different intelligences such as visual, kinesthetic, and active. If you have a student in your classroom that learns best from these three abilities, you should design a lesson that incorporates each ability, an activity that involves images, movement, and active learning.

When you harvest these abilities in your students and provide them a safe environment to experiment and make mistakes, they will develop into creative thinkers who are open-minded, adaptable, flexible, and experimental learners. Neuroscience has also provided some interesting information about the brain and learning by building on play and emotion. Play and emotion are needed for cognition to take place.

In order for learning to occur, a learning environment needs stimuli so students can explore and develop their natural curiosity for learning. As the teacher, you help with this process by designing thinking lessons that provide a mixture of complex and meaningful challenges that students can create something from.

LEARNING TAXONOMIES

Learning taxonomies is a map of sequences or skills that a learner must move through to achieve a specific process. Bloom's Taxonomy is a good example. Many educators use Bloom's Taxonomy when developing their learning objectives. Breaking the objectives down into these domains helps to organize student learning.

The focus of Bloom's Taxonomy is to build a lesson up from prerequisite knowledge and skills to constructing new concepts or ideas from students' prior knowledge and skills. By the end of the lesson, students should be able to synthesize information and create something new from it.

Bloom's Taxonomy was updated in 2000 by Anderson and Krathwohl (2001) to include creativity. With this change, creativity became the highest level of cognitive functioning a learner could achieve. When a learner created something new from the information studied, produced an original idea or product, it was then that the learner truly understood the problem.

As a teacher, it is necessary for you to create a community of inquiry. This is done through a classroom that supports the development of thinking and debate skills. An open community is formed that serves as a foundation for learning that encourages wondering, reasoning, and logic. As educators, we are also aware that specific criteria must be measured in order to determine the quality of one's thinking and this is done using a rubric.

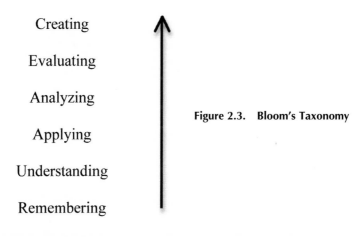

Figure 2.3.   Bloom's Taxonomy

When we consider a community of learners, we think about each learner learning from one another and questioning the ideas of others. This concept brings in the idea of authentic learning. When we engage our students by linking their interests into our content and then have students question one another's understanding, we have succeeded in bringing students into the learning process.

Marzano, Pickering, and Pollock (2001) identified strategies to help improve student understanding across content areas and grade levels. They determined that if we pull in graphic representations of our content, also known as graphic organizers, we can help students organize information, generate data, and then test their hypotheses.

Today, we continue to look at these ideas of community, authentic, and ubiquitous learning. All provide opportunities, resources, and constructive learning spaces for our students in order for them to better understand our content and, as a result, the world around them. These theorists all suggest that students develop skills in order to analyze authentic situations through inquiry and then develop an understanding through imagination and innovation.

In each classroom lesson, you want to incorporate higher-level thinking activities, visual representations, community of practice, inquiry, and ultimately innovative thinking to create flexible and adventurous thinkers. These are thinkers who are not afraid to take risks and who like being entrepreneurial in their thought processes.

PUTTING IT INTO PRACTICE

So if the idea behind creative thinking is for you to present open-ended and ambiguous questions so your students can be flexible and inventive thinkers . . . how exactly does that work?

Table 2.1.   Graphic Organizer for Identifying Problems and Solutions

Problem Chart	
Possible Problems	Possible Solutions

One way is to provide experiences around your learning goals so that students can practice each of these cognitive skills in a safe environment. They pull in information that is "messy" with the intent and focus of developing inventive thinking.

In various class activities, allow your students the ability to practice, receive feedback, and revisit content in multiple ways throughout the activity. For example, math has traditionally been taught by providing an equation and a few examples. This solves the issue of practice and feedback. However, when we are unable to provide multiple strategies for students to solve a math problem, we are not creating flexible or inventive thinking.

Developing adaptable and innovative thinkers requires providing students with multiple opportunities to recognize details in different patterns. From there, you provide them with an opportunity to explore these new patterns in order to help them transfer this knowledge to a more complex situation and to begin thinking creatively.

For example, your fifth-grade geometry class is learning about triangles. You have presented the equation and have suggested to your students how to figure out the outlined problems. Students work on a set of problems using the equation.

Now what? How can you build on this lesson to encourage students to see this lesson in a new way to build true understanding? To build inventive thinking?

What if you had students create a miniature town? You set specific guidelines, such as particular shapes and dimensions, building types for homes and businesses, the need for a park, etc.

As part of the activity, students are tasked with creating a map using GoogleSketchUp http://sketchup.google.com/. In the GoogleSketchUp program, students identify parallel streets, perpendicular streets, and streets that intersect all within a specific grid.

Throughout this activity, students are tasked with thinking differently about the geometry terms and concepts that they learned in your earlier lesson by using the equations and ideas in a new, different, and creative way. This creative-thinking activity provides students with a different perspective and reference point.

In creating the miniature town, students are able to develop a new dimension to their overall learning about basic geometry. They can apply what they learned, test their own hypotheses, and question the ideas of others and themselves. As an extension, you could ask your students to identify an analogy or create an interactive story about their town and the importance of geometry in the town's creation.

The idea behind creative thinking is to continually have your students build on their understanding in order to reorganize information and create a deeper, fuller knowledge base of the content and the real world around them.

Traditionally, we have taught students about the need for correct or incorrect answers. Right or wrong—with very little gray area or room for interpretation. For example, the equation for the perimeter of a rectangle is exact and must be written in a particular way.

As we begin to incorporate creative thinking into our curriculum, it is important to allow students to think differently about intended problems, such as an equation, and to provide meaningful experiences that incorporate different ways for students to arrive at an answer. In addition, we then want students to go further and build on that answer by testing it using different methods.

This can be difficult and is not an easy process, especially in a standards-based world. But it can be done. One way is to incorporate "what if" scenarios with varying solutions. Scenarios provide an opportunity for students to work on problems and determine different solutions.

For example, let's say that each morning, you get up and pour a glass of orange juice for breakfast. In the back of your mind you think, "This orange juice is too sweet." But each morning you continue to pour the orange juice into your glass without any adjustments.

The creative thinker walks into the same kitchen and pours a glass of orange juice and says, "Wow, this is sweet!" Immediately, this thinker determines possible solutions. After a few moments, he adds half a cup of water to the glass, takes a sip and says, "Yum, less sweet and it now has more orange flavor. Problem solved."

As a teacher, how can you move your students to this new paradigm shift? The idea that multiple solutions are possible? The first step is for you to begin thinking more creatively about your content so that you can help your students do the same.

MOVING BEYOND CRITICAL THINKING TO CREATIVE THINKING

As teachers, we design lessons that involve forms of critical thinking. Your lessons incorporate various forms of analysis such as:

- understanding claims made, e.g., the equation is stated as such, and this is how you place your numbers into it to find the correct answer; or
- the ability to follow and create a logical argument, e.g., the author stated this in the text, so what must happen next for the story to progress?

In each of these examples, you are working with specific thinking strategies that allow your students to determine one correct answer while eliminating the need for any alternative answer(s). How can we move from the obvious to the inventive? One way is to provide opportunities for your students to explore a variety of ideas and possible solutions before deciding on a response.

For example, your next lesson looks at the Revolutionary War. Your students have learned all of the key events and terms in this lesson because you have aligned your unit with the state standards. You decide that you want students to take their understanding to a new level and create a "slam poem" (a poem performed for a live audience) about the Revolutionary War.

The class is divided into small groups. One group looks at the Revolutionary War from the colonists' perspective and another group looks at the Revolutionary War from England's perspective. You have just pushed students' understanding of the Revolutionary War a step further, forcing them to be inventive and creative.

Both critical and creative thinking are important tools to help students develop the necessary skills needed to learn about various events in history, such as the Revolutionary War. Through this class activity, students are able to question perspectives, discover factual information by looking at primary-source data, and think about issues of the time period and how these issues helped form a new world.

When you ask students to now take this new information and write a poem from a different perspective, you build on their new knowledge gained of the Revolutionary War.

CHAPTER SUMMARY

In designing your lessons, you want to incorporate inquiry skills that involve higher-level questioning, as well as create an environment that involves creative thinking and innovative thought. The following is a visual of this idea.

As you think about creative thinking, it is often helpful to think about it as "divergent" thinking. You are building on one's thoughts and ideas through imagining or inventing something new, with the optimum goal of generating new ideas out of one's existing ideas.

In Bloom's Taxonomy, this would be considered synthesis: The ability to take what is understood and create a new product or a new view; the ability of your students to take a broad idea and break it down into its smallest parts so they can rebuild it into something entirely different. Thus, they are producing original thinking and imaginative ideas around an old problem.

Creative Thinking   Critical Thinking

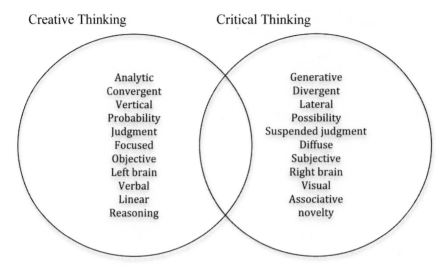

Figure 2.4.   **Critical and Creative Thinking**

As we see in Bloom's Taxonomy, words often associated with synthesis include: compose, construct, design, revise, create, formulate, produce, and plan. In order to develop this in your classroom, you must ask questions that go beyond factual answers.

Creative thinkers of today include Steve Jobs, the former CEO of Apple Inc. Jobs was an inventive designer and ultimately a creative thinker. Throughout his career at Apple, he was able to look at the standard electronic device of his time and make it different. Better. Beyond what users could imagine or even knew that they wanted. That is innovation and what we are trying to foster in our students of today.

CHAPTER REFLECTION

1. What is the difference between "inquiry" thinking and "creative" thinking?
2. How does theory impact the teaching practice?
3. How can you challenge your students to think differently about learning?
4. What does a successful thinking curriculum look like?
5. How will you reinvent lessons to help your students become creative thinkers in your content area? List three specific examples and provide details of each lesson.
6. Build an inquiry-learning activity into your lesson that incorporates creative thinking. Identify how technology will be used to build deeper connections for each student.

Chapter Three

Embedding Information Literacy into Your Course

There is a need for students to be information literate in today's fast-moving global society. This chapter explores information literacy and provides approaches teachers can take to incorporate this important skill into student lessons and activities.

OVERVIEW

Information literacy is a skill that is expected of students once they leave school. The rationale behind this required skill is that students should be able to sift through vast amounts of information created daily in our information-centric society to determine its effectiveness and quality and then reformat that information into new and meaningful knowledge that others can learn from.

The ideas of critical thinking, problem solving, and creative expression are central to this skill. Your students must possess each to be information literate. Teaching students to develop and build these cognitive skills by determining how information is organized, how to find quality information, evaluate different types of information, and then create new information for others to access and learn from is the goal.

Today, in this information age, learning how to learn and how to *think* is fundamental. Students need information literacy skills in order to obtain economic and personal success. Over 70 percent of American workers engage with information in their jobs. Because of the importance placed on information and knowledge by our global society, students need to develop information literacy skills that enable them to perform specific methods and strategies to work with information to be successful.

Creating a learning environment that is interactive and allows for self-initiated learning will help you facilitate this process. Teaching your students to think about the content they are studying in new and different ways, by asking good questions, and finding credible information is an important goal.

Technology is a tool that can be incorporated into your information literacy activity to allow students to search, discover, simulate, and manipulate information so that they can critically and creatively think about the information, moving beyond just memorizing facts.

As students evaluate information to determine its relevancy, they also begin creating organizational structures for the information they are collecting so they can begin to manipulate and apply it in new and meaningful ways. This ability stretches their creative thinking to a new level.

As students locate, evaluate, and collect information that they believe will help them answer meaningful questions, they begin to cultivate this important skill in dynamic ways. They focus not only on the content in front of them, but on expanding their overall views about the topics being studied into a new process of understanding. They move beyond just the basic facts to more conceptual understanding of the new knowledge.

This process of accessing, evaluating, and then using information becomes an important element in creating meaning for your students. This is the only way they will be able to understand complex concepts, opinions, and ideas. To help in this process, it is important that you teach students what quality information looks like and how to ask important questions of the content to develop deeper understanding.

Gardner's (2009) theory of multiple intelligences is a good way to introduce students to these important skills. As you design lessons to enhance students' information literacy skills, you also want to consider ways your students learn best and then develop specific strategies for them to begin locating good information.

Keeping this in mind, look for primary, secondary, Internet, databases, and print resources to include in your lessons. Incorporating images, letters, numerical values, maps, and video allows you to begin modeling best practices to your students. This also provides them with dynamic and relevant resource-based learning experiences to develop and refine their own thinking and information collection skills.

When thinking about incorporating rich and relevant resource-based materials into your lessons, think about ways you can incorporate collaboration and problem solving into the activity so students have an opportunity to develop critical-thinking skills in guided practice. Working in an inquiry-rich-oriented environment, such as groups, resembles authentic experiences that enable students to solve complex problems.

As introduced in chapters one and two, Bloom's Taxonomy provides a framework to create a lesson that allows students to begin developing higher-order thinking skills and creativity around complex problems. During the lesson, you want to continue to model well-organized practice in locating appropriate information sources and asking important questions during the learning process.

As the lesson develops, ask students questions to allow them to think about how they can apply their new understanding about the found information. They are then able to use information from answered questions around the overarching problem in order to create something new. This new information can be used to help others as well as themselves.

By using this new understanding to create a product or an emerging idea and extending your activity to this higher level, you allow students to scaffold their understanding from prior learning.

This scaffolding and new form of information manipulation provides an opportunity for students to create an even deeper understanding of the context of the information and the problem itself. This deeper understanding can then be transferred into new knowledge, whether it be through a newly developed product or a new process.

Only when your students do something meaningful with information is knowledge created at a deeper level. Doing something means manipulation, thinking about it in new and different ways, and critically critiquing or analyzing it, all to synthesize the information so it can be transformed into something original for others.

GETTING STARTED

It is important not to compartmentalize information literacy within what we already know of literacy. Instead, think of information literacy as inclusive of literacy. As you incorporate literacy into your classroom, begin to consider information literacy as a building block to overall literacy.

Information literacy means that you are able to:

- Recognize the need for good information to solve problems and generate ideas.
- Formulate higher-order questions that identify your specific information needs.
- Integrate prior knowledge with new information to build understanding around complex topics and ideas.
- Find diverse information with varying views and reference sources.

- Use strategies that allow you to identify effective search terms to narrow search results.
- Create organized systems around information.
- Use new information critically and resourcefully in order to solve complex problems that may not have clear or previously defined solutions.

We are currently experiencing a shift in the ecology of obtaining knowledge. Google, http://www.google.com, a popular search engine, provides a wide span of information in a few search seconds. A simple search can find blog posts giving the searcher up-to-the-minute information on topics that are popular. Wikipedia, http://en.wikipedia.org/wiki/Main_Page, an online encyclopedia, can also provide information on specific topics providing a good starting point for any researcher.

Research journals and databases provide both original and primary-source documents that the information seeker can use to obtain data and a broader view of information. In each information source, different types of information are utilized to help students question and discover new knowledge.

As a teacher, how do you help your students learn from these types of resources? How do you help them sift through the vast amount of information to find quality resources? One way is to introduce search engines. As a class, ask important questions of information found in your search. Questions such as:

- What does ranking mean in a Web search?
- Why should phrases be used when conducting a search?
- Are all search engines the same?
- What makes a Web site an authority on a topic?
- How do I find primary sources?

In order for students to become information literate they must be able to ask tough questions of any information source they encounter. One important lesson is the difficulty in verifying information found online as being accurate.

So, let's give it a try. If you are doing this in your class, include Web resources that are relevant to your content. For this example, we are going to use the Web site News of the Weird, at http://www.newsoftheweird.com/.

Introduce this activity to students by letting them know that it is important to really question information found online for both quality and appeal. Access the Web site News of the Weird. Browse around the site and read a couple of postings. Ask the question: *Are these stories true?*

Have students explain their responses. After students have had a chance to explain their reasoning, place them in small groups, approximately three people per group. Assign each of the groups one news story from the Web site. Ask them to verify that the stories are true.

As students conduct research, they will find that the stories can be verified by news media outlets. Ask students if this new revelation—that these stories have been printed in newspapers—proves that they are true. Why is it important to determine if a story is true? What are good resources that will help you determine if a news story is true?

If you have access to the database LexisNexis, look up the news stories identified to track down wire service reports. Let students know that, yes, News of the Weird is a quality Internet source. This Web site is a good example of the difficulties searchers have when finding and verifying the accuracy of information found online. Using other resources to help verify a found source is an important and necessary information skill.

Next, introduce another Web site. As a class, visit the Urban Legends Web site at http://urbanlegends.about.com/. Discuss the legend with your students. Use the information found on the About Us page to explain how this site verifies the urban legends identified on the Web site.

As a class, discuss the nature of the information found on the Web site and the ease with which this information circulated. Discuss the need to critically examine information found online and the need to use a variety of resources, to understand the nature of the source, and to look to others, such as librarians and specific research collections, to help focus searches and find relevant and accurate sources.

A CHANGE IN CURRICULUM PACE

As you incorporate more complexity into your lessons—by moving into a thinking pedagogy from a solely direct instruction pedagogy—the curriculum for your students begins to come to life. As you think critically about the curriculum, you will find yourself more inclined to begin developing questions that engage your students with the "messy" real-life problems that are centered around creative or divergent thinking in our everyday world.

When you introduce problems that are muddled around your lesson objectives, rather than problems that are neat and well labeled with clear and distinct answers, your students will begin to look beyond prepackaged materials for correct answers to a variety of resources that they can critically think about to determine the best solutions.

Your main goal in this type of inquiry activity is to have students present you with more than one correct answer, just like they would do in real life. Instead of one specific correct answer, real-world problems oftentimes have many possible answers and can be untidy. When we try to solve a "messy" problem from an information literate perspective, we must be able to review a variety of sources that contain many alternative solutions and determine what will work best.

In your classroom, identify specific methods to help students become better questioners of information. Design lessons that help students identify a specific problem, formulate effective search strategies that incorporate appropriate keywords, and begin asking questions to help students find applicable resources.

Once information is found, students must have the skill set to evaluate the diverse information to determine if it is credible and solves the intended problem. By helping to develop this skill structure for students, you help them achieve the necessary thinking skills that can be transferred across the curriculum.

Information literacy skills move beyond the Internet, but when looking for quality resources to help solve real-world problems, information such as primary sources (images, letters, research studies, government statistics and documents) can be readily available and found on the Web. Good research skills are necessary to help students understand bias and how to ask good questions in order to find credible information.

In this process, your goal is to create lessons and activities that allow students to dig deeper into your content, whether you are teaching math, science, literature, writing, reading, art, or physical education. All of the content taught in schools has core understandings, e.g., what we want students to walk away with when they leave the class.

Create a learning environment that encourages students to take a critical look at these core understandings and seek appropriate information to work through problems to comprehend the meaning intended at a deeper level. Simply delivering information on our part is not good enough. Not for a 21st-century learner.

Instead, we need to provide opportunities for students to think about what is important and will help them on any standardized test or life problem that they encounter. As you incorporate rich and dynamic resources to help encourage your students, they too will use these resources and then advance to finding resources on their own. It is important to encourage them to be curious about your topic.

As an example, let's begin by selecting appropriate resources to answer a problem. To introduce the activity, ask students where they find information about a movie, the weather for a weekend sports game, or a political figure. Have students notice that information can come from a variety of resources such as newspapers, books, and scholarly journals, as well as popular Internet sites.

Place your students into small groups and ask them the following question: *What were the major causes of World War II?*

Identify two information sources that would help them find the answer. Come together as a group and have students share their answers. Have students determine what are good sources for this topic and what are not.

As you identify good resources and introduce students to other possible sources that could help them determine the answer to this problem, ask them about keywords. What are they and why are they important?

In a related example, as a group, view the Georgia O'Keeffe Museum at http://www.okeeffemuseum.org/art-exhibitions.html. Ask students to identify and call out all the words and phrases they would use to describe the artist. The point is that many different words or phrases can be used for one idea, topic, or person. When your students keyword search, they should tap into their prior knowledge and pull up as many different words or phrases as possible.

PREPARING INFORMATION LITERATE STUDENTS

Helping students become information literate by using their own intellectual curiosity should be a goal in all of your lesson designs. The idea of incorporating activities that will teach students how to think, access, evaluate, and use information in efficient, effective, critical, creative, and ethical ways will help enhance and foster this curiosity.

In each lesson, have students find good information and then use that information in some way. Even when they are determining the quality of a resource, you want them to work with the information and think about it in new ways so that they can discover something from it.

For example, go to the Web site http://www.dhmo.org/ and ask your students the following: *Should we ban dihydrogen monoxide?*

Give them time to explore the Web site and determine an answer by providing support. From this activity, students can see that they must go deeper than a Web URL to determine what is a quality or a misleading resource. They must look beyond the top five Web sites that are listed in their favorite search engine to find a credible source.

Continue this discussion by asking students to give an example of a selection process they use in everyday life, such as how they choose a movie, a piece of clothing, a lunch choice, or buying a music CD. Illustrate to students that their selection process is similar to the research process in general. Just as they have criteria on what to eat for lunch, for example, so too should they establish criteria for Internet resources that they deem credible.

They should ask questions about the source itself, by identifying the person or group responsible for the Web site and identifying the credentials of this individual or group by looking at the About Us page or Contact Us page.

They should also be able to discern the purpose of the Web site or resource. Is it to inform, persuade, sell, or entertain? Next, what about the content? Has it been updated? Is the information presented in a nonbiased way or is there some commercial intent built in? Is it free from errors? Is it professionally presented?

To help illustrate this point, pose a question to your students, such as: *What are the latest findings on the public's concerns regarding global warming?*

Display the following two Web sites: http://www.nws.noaa.gov and http://www.4cleanair.org/. Which Web site provides the most accurate coverage to answer this question? Which Internet resource would you prefer students use?

A second illustration can be seen with the questions: *When and where was Christopher Columbus born? What was he best known for?* Review http://www.biography.com/people/christopher-columbus-9254209/ and http://allaboutexplorers.com/explorers/columbus/. Which Web site does a better job of answering the questions posed?

Some good Internet sites for students to learn more about the importance of evaluating Web pages include:

• Need Help, How to Spot a Fake Web site, found at http://report-online -scams.com/how-to-spot-a-fake-website/
• Intentionally Misleading Web Sites, available at http://www.techlearning .com/article/intentionally-misleading-web-sites/42539

A good Web site for you to use as the teacher about this topic is:

• Teacher Tap: Evaluating Internet Resources, located at http://eduscapes .com/tap/topic32.htm

Technology Tools to Help with Curriculum

Integrating technology is a difficult task. Often we use technology in our classrooms to simply present information. It can be used at a deeper, more critical level. We can use technology to become literate about copyright laws, write and communicate in more diverse ways across a variety of mediums, develop note-taking and synthesizing skills, and appreciate creative expressions.

When you design your lesson and think about how to integrate technology to enhance a particular topic or necessary skill-development task, think about what you want your students to do and how the technology tool can help in the process.

Before introducing what you want your students to uncover and develop, you need to be knowledgeable of your pedagogy, content, and the technology itself. A good knowledge of technology entails understanding how various types of technology can change your teaching and enhance student learning.

As you already know, there are a variety of technology tools available and each of these tools work for specific tasks. It is important to understand these tasks and specific tool relationships so you can choose the appropriate tool for a particular task or even the one that best suits your teaching or pedagogy.

Think about how you can best use the technology tools that will allow students to understand a particular topic, problem, or issue as it relates to their diverse interests and abilities. You also want to consider the best ways that technology can help you evaluate student understanding.

DIGITAL STORYTELLING
TO ENHANCE INFORMATION LITERACY

Digital storytelling is one method that can be used to incorporate technology into your lesson so students can practice skills that they learned. They can then transfer this new knowledge to an active and original understanding in their own life.

Digital storytelling involves creating a story using technology tools and skills. It also has the ability to enhance communication skills, collaboration skills, verbal skills, creativity, visual and auditory literacy, information literacy skills, and project management skills.

A good digital story requires that students move through the lesson and garner a good understanding of both the content and the essential question. From this, they can then find good resources to help support their solution to the question posed. Students identify important facts and ideas that they can utilize to tell the story and use text, images, and animation.

To determine whether students understand the main idea of the lesson, allow them to create a digital story by finding quality resources and then use those resources to convey understanding of the topic. Think of a digital story as a way for students to communicate meaning from the lesson through writing, researching, and presenting information.

Before your students are able to create their own digital story, they must have a deep understanding of the topic itself. They must also have a creative story that they can tell. Their story must have an audience and must be presented in a new and novel way.

The purpose of a digital story is not for students to regurgitate information from one source into another source. This is not a complex, cognitive skill. Instead, the purpose is for students to present their new knowledge about a topic or problem in an interesting way in order to convey a message or solve a particular problem.

Within the process of completing a digital story, students work in small groups to research, sift, organize, write, rewrite, collect relevant artifacts, and compile each part into a meaningful and purposeful message. Through the entire process, students build on their foundational literacy skills.

The narrative of the digital story allows students to put a voice to their understanding for an identified audience. This written script helps to test student understanding as a group and to determine what works and what does not work in order to convey the most important information in a select amount of time.

Students develop this script through their research and resources. As they finish their script, review and rewrite, they begin their voiceover and start recording.

The voiceover is a main part of the story. As they add images and text to the screen, students develop emotion around their message. This is an important part of the overall digital story and to developing information literacy skills.

This step is where the story becomes more personal for students and eventually personal for the audience themselves. The voice of the story is a way in which the viewer experiences the message your students have developed and their personal understanding.

Group work is an integral part of the process, and teaching students the skills needed to work successfully in teams is essential. In groups, each member should have a specific role and task to complete. Within each of these specific roles and tasks, encourage your students to be both innovative and creative.

Small groups allow each member to become an author, finding and designing information to communicate a specific understanding through images, animation, and voice; they also allow a team member to work with others to create something that has not been created before or to solve a specific problem.

This unique opportunity of digital storytelling allows the group to work together to mix different media in order to create something that did not exist before.

When designing a digital story activity, organize students with different story prompts around specific points in your topic that you expect them to understand. Your lesson should focus on student questioning along with opportunities for research and discovery. All of this is focused on students providing a culminating product, a good story premise.

For example, if you are teaching a lesson on the Civil War, have students identify key issues relating to the war and how these issues impacted society at the time. Have students locate key resources and then share their findings with the class.

As you introduce the digital story part of the lesson, take their new knowledge and what they found to a different level. Have them create a digital story that relates to their personal life or an influence of their personal thinking as it relates to today.

When students plan for this complex type of story, they move away from reporting on facts about information they gathered during the lesson to a level of personal reflection on both their own engagement with the content and how the subject relates to their current world. A leading question for their story might be: *Describe an event that you studied about the Civil War and how this specific event relates to your community today.*

This statement requires your students to deepen their overall understanding of issues surrounding the Civil War and the issues that surround them today by asking them to share their new understanding. In other words, the digital story is a reflection of "what they learned," as well as a relatedness to their own personal view of life through "why it is important."

This exercise forces your students to think. They think about how facts about events can influence their own thinking or beliefs, even today. The creation of their digital story forces them to think differently about the facts that they learned in the lesson, to reflect more deeply on both their cognitive and personal engagement with the content, and to move beyond factual knowledge.

INFORMATION LITERACY IN YOUR LESSON

When you are teaching a topic like the Civil War, you want students to gain a core understanding about issues that divided the nation, specific events and battles, leaders that emerged, the daily life of citizens, and the aftermath of the war itself.

Each of these topics includes several subtopics. Each topic and subtopic has its own information resource attached. Ensure that you provide students with detailed information, primary-source photos, and documents to help them discover answers to complex problems.

To help students understand the importance of information, you want to identify and demonstrate throughout the lesson that all of the information within your lesson was carefully researched. One way you could do this is by providing your students with the evaluation measures you used for each resource.

See Kathy Schrock's Critical Evaluation Surveys at http://www.schrock guide.net/critical-evaluation.html and ABC's of Web site Evaluation at http://kathyschrock.net/abceval/ for assistance on determining good Web sites.

Modeling and demonstrating good practice is important in any lesson. But, it is especially important when you expect your students to find good information.

Throughout your lesson, provide mini-activities around key topics: for example, the different views of the North and South, abolitionists, leaders, and/or specific artifacts that students can explore to come up with a good understanding of the Civil War. Encourage questioning when students look at these resources by providing them with "What Would You Do?" scenarios.

The main premise is to teach students to think about resources when generating ideas and solutions to problems. During the lesson, identify key words and have your students create an index to help organize and define these words. Your students can use these key words for their own research to help them build their digital story. The entire lesson, all the way up to the digital story, is a building block.

After your lesson, engage students in critical thinking by navigating and collecting information from primary-source Web sites that includes letters written by soldiers and policies led by government officials. Students will see that resources can provide a personal view that may be very different from that written in popular literature. During this entire process, through the lessons researched and resources gathered, students learn about the Civil War.

Once each of these mini-activities is completed, students can work in small groups to explore a person or issue further to create a digital story. The creation of their story will require them to work together, to think deeply and critically about the issues they have studied, and to relate this understanding to a personal feeling, view, or event of today.

They do this by telling a story and using technology tools and multiple media elements to communicate to others in a meaningful, thoughtful way. This type of activity requires your students to be flexible, take initiative, and produce something creative.

CHAPTER SUMMARY

Information literacy is an essential skill for students to grasp. It is a process through which they find, understand, evaluate, and use information in various formats in order to create new information for their personal, social, and/or global purposes.

In order for students to develop this skill, they must gain experience in exploring and questioning issues and concerns within complex and authentic problems, find and then use quality and diverse information from relevant sources, synthesize complex information into manageable chunks, and then tie this information into their existing knowledge in order to solve the problem posed and create new knowledge that others can learn from.

CHAPTER REFLECTION

1. How is information literacy an extension of literacy?
2. What specific ways can you incorporate information literacy and higher-order thinking into your lessons?
3. What specific resources are important for students to learn content?

SKILL BUILDING ACTIVITY

Throughout this chapter, you explored how to create a lesson that incorporates information literacy. The focus was on engaging students to think critically about the variety of resources they will use to solve complex problems. Now it is your turn to create a lesson or activity that frames a specific query around a lesson objective. As you think about an activity, incorporate some of the elements below into your lesson:

- Identify a complex problem around your lesson objective that students should solve.
- Have students ask clarifying questions and create research questions.
- Have students identify specific information that they will need to solve their problem. (Asking questions: What do I need to know? What kind of information should I gather? What information do I already know? What gaps in knowledge do I have?)
- Introduce a Concept Map, such as a graphic technique to organize their informational needs.
- Have students identify information from a variety of sources and assess specific information within individual resources.
- Have students identify search terms they will use to find specific information.
- Have students organize information found in meaningful and logical ways.
- Have students take notes to help understand the information through comments and reflection.
- Share findings in an effective way, complying with copyright laws and issues of intellectual property.

Chapter Four

Setting Up an Activity:
Tying Good Questions to Objectives

In chapters one through three, you were introduced to inquiry-oriented learning, creative thinking, and information literacy. The importance of a "big idea" question and the need for meaningful activities to ensure students are achieving understanding as well as creating meaning from each task were introduced.

In chapter four, we explore how to write objectives, specifically the need to identify meaningful learning objectives in order to design an inquiry-oriented lesson that incorporates creative thinking and embeds information literacy.

OVERVIEW

The premise of inquiry learning is that students assume a lead role in their own learning. This is similar to the constructivist's view of teaching and learning. In adopting this approach, teachers may get the impression that creating instructional objectives is unnecessary. If students are in charge of their own learning, then why do teachers need to identify goals and objectives? The very opposite is true.

When inquiry learning is integrated into your classroom, planning must be a priority in the process. Goals and objectives need to be identified, lesson plans developed, quality resources found, and a "big idea" question developed. In setting the stage and completing these preparatory steps, students have a better understanding of the learning process and the content, and are therefore more engaged and ready to embark on their learning experience.

PLANNING STAGE

Each part of an inquiry-oriented activity should serve a purpose and have clear goals. Planning is the first step in the inquiry process. Throughout your design process, you should always go back to your objectives to ensure that you are creating a learning activity that is on task with your stated goals. This helps to ensure the outcome and that your students are engaged in an activity that is authentic and relevant.

When creating an inquiry-oriented activity, it is important for students to take the lead, but there must be a clear path with well identified strategies to allow them to be successful and explore topics beyond the simple fact-finding missions of the past. One way to do this is to identify what you want students to understand from the activity and what you want them to "take away" in terms of knowledge gained.

Objectives and assessments can then be identified to ensure that students remain on task and are able to articulate why the lesson is important and what goals are necessary for them to achieve. By identifying these critical "takeaways," you begin to think about essential learning outcomes and how relationships can be developed and built on main concepts.

This is accomplished by looking at the standards of learning (SOLs) for your topic and deciphering what the big picture is and how best to identify the importance of this picture to your students.

For example, below are two SOLs. Identify the takeaway from each.

Standards of Learning:

- SOL1: Using appropriate technology, students will solve problems in mathematics.
- SOL2: Students will represent and interpret the relationships between quantities algebraically.

Takeaway:

- Technology can aid in solving these types of algebraic problems.
- Variables, such as x and y, can be used to represent unknown quantities in algebraic expressions.

Next, learning objectives can be written that identify what students will understand and the resultant takeaway from the lesson.

After identifying both the takeaway and the objective for each SOL, provide opportunities for students to dig deeper into the content. Instructional

Table 4.1.   Learning Objectives

Students will:
• Use spreadsheet software to simulate algebraic expressions and post their reflections on the class blog to share with experts in the field of mathematics.

Students will:
• Compare and contrast numeric and algebraic expressions.
• Evaluate algebraic expressions, given that the value represented by variables (non-numeric letters) represents the unknown.
• Write a real-world problem to represent the algebraic expression.

strategies can be created that allow students to think critically about the concepts by analyzing and exploring various algebraic expressions. The new knowledge and understanding of mathematical variables gained can then be presented in meaningful ways.

The following is a sample activity in a mathematics classroom:

In a large group discussion, introduce new concepts of mathematical variables and algebraic expressions.

Goal: Introduce the meaning of this new algebraic language to students and connect this language to their personal lives.

Activity: Have students write down something they are wearing, such as jeans or tennis shoes. This will be their value of expression.
Then, as a group identify variables for each article identified.
For example:
n = necklace
w = watch
s = shirt
j = jeans

Ask students to raise their hands if they wrote down jeans as their value of expression. Write the number next to j. Repeat with necklaces, watches, and shirts.

5j   6n   10w   8s

Through this activity the importance of variables has been determined and students are now beginning to identify reasons and application for the mathematical expressions.

The expression, 5j, is not simply "5j"; rather it represents in mathematical form five students in the class who identified jeans as the item of clothing they are wearing.

Figure 4.1.   Sample Activity

The main point of this exercise is to:

(a) Identify SOLs;
(b) Determine the takeaway, for each SOL; and
(c) Establish learning objectives for each.

A follow-up example is provided below on a lesson concerning the U.S. Constitution:

Responsibility of the teacher:
Identify why the study of the U.S. Constitution and three branches of government is important for students and what is central for them to understand.

Questions to consider:
- What are the most important concepts for students to understand from this unit?
- What is important for students to remember about this unit a year from now?
- What observable behaviors do I want students to demonstrate and which cognitive domains will be evident?

Figure 4.2. Sample Questions

By identifying what is important about the lesson, the teacher is able to break down the unit into meaningful learning tasks and ultimately essential questions. For example, in the above illustration it is important that students know the three branches of government and how each branch of government is tied to the U.S. Constitution and to them as citizens.

Once the teacher identifies what is important for students to understand, then a "big idea" question can be identified and necessary objectives of the lesson established. Objectives are the road map for students to take; they stipulate how students will identify and explore the "big idea" question.

To begin identifying an objective, you must first identify a learning standard. It is at this stage that you should also think about which technology tool can be used to enhance student learning during the exploration and presentation of new knowledge.

Table 4.2 provides an outline of the process for this example.

As stated above, objectives provide a road map for students to answer the "big idea" question. This road map is not limited, but instead provides a structure to help students develop a good understanding of the "big idea" question and know what the expectations are for the lesson and what is important to understand at the completion of the lesson.

Table 4.2. Identifying the Objective and Big Idea Question

Topic:	*U.S. Constitution and the Three Branches of Government*
Standards:	The student will demonstrate knowledge of the American constitutional government by:
	• Explaining the relationship of state governments to the national government in the federal system;
	• Describing the structure and powers of local, state, and national governments; and
	• Explaining the principle of separation of powers and the operation of checks and balances by identifying the procedures for amending the U.S. Constitution
	The student will use technology to locate, evaluate, and collect information from a variety of sources.
	The student will use technology resources for solving problems and making informed decisions.
Goal:	Students will understand how the Constitution of the United States impacts citizens. They will do this through interviews, analyzing primary source documents, and using digital images, video, and sound files to tell a story about how the U.S. Constitution plays a role in their lives.
Objective:	Using primary source documents, design a story about the three branches of the U.S. Government and how each branch impacts your day-to-day life in the United States.
Big Idea Question:	How are the U.S. Constitution and the three branches of government related to each other?
Technology Tools:	Example technology tools that could engage students in answering these questions:
	• A MindMap Tool to highlight and provide a visual of the major concepts identified between branches of government and the U.S. Constitution.
	• Online database housing primary sources (images, letters, the Constitution, sound files, video) to read the Constitution of the United States and to review images of places and artifacts.
	• Multimedia (video, Web authoring, hyperstudio, podcasting) to combine artifacts, findings, and analysis to present understandings.
	• A Web site to post a presentation for parents and other students in different locations to view and ask questions about.

When you provide an open-ended "big idea" question, students are provided with an opportunity to explore the topic in depth. It also has potential for students to dig deeper into the content and go beyond a general understanding of the topic. When teachers provide clear objectives and learning goals, they provide a clear path for students to take in their inquiry task.The idea of an inquiry-oriented activity is to go beyond the knowledge domain outlined by Bloom, the educational theorist discussed earlier in this book. Bloom outlined the taxonomy of learning objectives and important steps to get students moving toward higher-order thinking skills such as application, analysis, synthesis, and evaluation of content as they work on classroom activities.

Objectives should identify these skills and highlight what the expectations are for each student. For example, an inquiry-oriented objective for the above activity in a third-grade class could be as follows:

The student will create a coloring book identifying and explaining each branch of government, how each branch checks and balances one another, and the relationship of the three government branches to the U.S. Constitution. When complete, the coloring book will be posted on the class Web site for other classes to learn from.

THE INQUIRY PROCESS: QUESTIONS TO CONSIDER

In developing a lesson centered on the U.S. Constitution, questions need to be carefully considered by you, the teacher, when designing the inquiry activity. This ensures that the inquiry process is achieved for each student and the class as a whole.

1. Identify and list the specific skills you want students to develop when working on an inquiry-oriented activity.
   a. Do you want students to practice and develop research skills?
   b. What steps should students take when synthesizing information gathered?
   c. What strategies will you provide students so that they have the necessary skills for research and synthesis?
   d. How will the specific skills and knowledge relate to the identified learning standards and lesson objectives?
   e. How will students work as a collaborative group?
2. What built-in methods will you use to evaluate student understanding throughout the lesson?
   a. How will you and your students collect data and information to provide an overview of student learning?

b. What questions can you ask students throughout the activity to ensure they are on track and are learning what is intended?

3. How will you provide a real-world experience that gives students the opportunity to explore the "big" idea question of the activity?

   a. In the Constitution example, primary-source documents can be used to provide students with a real-world context that gives them the same tools a historian would use to solve such a problem.

   b. What strategies would help students reinforce this new understanding? Determine how a historian would investigate this "big idea" question and then provide students with opportunities to build these same skills.

   c. Introduce the question by having students brainstorm about the laws in their community, state, and the U.S. government.

   d. Encourage students to think about past lessons by having them complete a KWL (What I Know) Chart.

   e. What types of technology tools will enhance student understanding?

4. Identify quality resources that provide students with the necessary information to explore the "big idea" question and help them develop a good understanding of the overall goal of the lesson itself.

   a. Are the resources appropriate for the identified learning standards and objectives?

   b. Will the resources help students solve the "big idea" question effectively?

5. Identify any distractions or problems that students may encounter when they work on the inquiry-oriented activity. Whether the distractors are new terms, complex resources, or new ideas, you want to work through possible strategies to overcome these potential problems to ensure that students succeed in their inquiry task. Determine the abilities of your students, such as knowledge of the subject, level of research skills, and overall understanding of the task.

   a. Is this activity appropriate for my students?

   b. Develop strategies to ensure that all students are successful in the activity.

Table 4.3 provides a template to note key questions and issues for you to consider when designing your inquiry-oriented activity.

At the conclusion of the inquiry-oriented activity, your students should be able to identify what was significant about the "big idea" question and how this new knowledge can be applied to past and future lessons. At the end of the lesson, students should also identify any confusion or disagreements they have with the information and be able to articulate how this new knowledge relates to their personal experiences.

Table 4.3.   Key Questions Template

Questions to Consider Based on Your Inquiry Development Activity	
Specific big ideas you want your students to achieve:	For example, English teachers may want students to be fluent in language. Big Idea Question: How do authors use different elements of a story to create mood?
Methods of evaluation (informal and formal):	What would be sufficient for my students to perform to demonstrate their understanding? Develop a brochure to help younger students understand what is meant by different elements of a story used by authors to create mood. Ask questions and observe to ensure students are thinking about the big idea question and are on task.
Real world experiences you will provide:	How can I incorporate relevancy into my unit? Students can create a wiki book highlighting understandings. Authors can comment and participate through the invitation of students.
Resources you have reviewed:	What resources can I provide to engage students in the important concepts I want them to discover? ReadWriteThink.org Character Graphic Organizers Worksheet Story Moods Graphic Organizer Worksheet Young Authors Narrative Conference Wikispaces.org
Distractions your students may encounter:	What types of distractions will students encounter to prevent understanding of the big idea question posed? Students may only remember topics studied but not understand the importance of the different concepts of mood and storytelling. Make sure activities focus students on important concepts.

TECHNOLOGY TOOLS AND THE "BIG IDEA" INVESTIGATION

The main rationale for integrating technology into an inquiry-oriented activity is to provide opportunities for students to experience and explore topics in a real-world context. It also helps with application.

Exploring a library database to find resources and search terms aids students in answering the "big idea" question. Critically evaluating resources found on the Internet to determine their credibility and reliability before using the information in a presentation helps students form critical analysis skills.

Additionally, students can analyze raw data found on the Internet at government Web sites, such as the U.S. Census Bureau or National Oceanic and Atmospheric Association (NOAA) to place in a spreadsheet or word processing program to answer outlined questions. Or alternatively, experts can be contacted at the Census Bureau and NOAA to help clarify specific questions students encounter from their data manipulation. In each of these examples, technology is used as a tool to communicate, research, analyze, and ultimately present new information.

In the chapters that follow, further exploration into inquiry-oriented activities utilizing technology will be provided. Specifically, we will look at creating a WebQuest, Web inquiry, telecollaborative, and problem-based activities using the Internet and technology tools to engage students in the process of learning.

CHAPTER SUMMARY

In this chapter, we explored the importance of ensuring that your learning objectives and learning goals were the central theme of your inquiry activity. As the teacher, you must have a clear understanding of what is important for students to understand and then be able to create a good "big idea" question around that intended understanding. You also want to provide relevancy to the activity by tying in authentic connections to the learning goal and tasks.

Next, you want to make sure you incorporate good teaching strategies as well as constructive feedback and reflection to ensure that students remain focused, engaged, and on task. Finally, you want to integrate technology tools into the activity to provide real-world relevancy and application for students. Technology can be utilized for communication, research, analysis, and presentation.

CHAPTER REFLECTION

1. Determine a "big idea" question that you can use for your next lesson.
2. Identify Standards of Learning (SOLs) that align with your "big idea" question.

3. List objectives to provide students with a road map to this "big idea" question and highlight your standard.
4. Identify the cognitive domains students will acquire while working on this activity.
5. Identify possible misunderstandings students may have in this inquiry-oriented activity.
6. Determine teaching strategies to aid students in their overall understanding of the "big idea" question.

SKILL-BUILDING ACTIVITY

Throughout chapter four we explored inquiry and how inquiry is built upon a "big idea" question. The central focus was on engaging students in an interesting and doable question that they are motivated to critically think about and to discover new information. Your goal at the conclusion of this chapter is to create a "big idea" question that aligns with your learning standards and is developed around an interesting and doable problem that really grabs the interest of your students.

Chapter Five

Creating a WebQuest

Over the past several years, WebQuests have been very popular in education. What exactly are they? A WebQuest is an inquiry-oriented activity where most if not all of the resources that your students explore and analyze are provided on the Internet. The goal of a WebQuest is to provide students with opportunities to explore content in meaningful and engaging ways.

A WebQuest should grab students' attention and take them on an interesting "quest" through a topic. A WebQuest can vary in length from short and concise to long and detailed. It is generally used to introduce a topic or have students tie together understanding at the end of a learning unit.

A WebQuest is not a static activity whereby students memorize facts or write a research report. Rather, it is an active learning activity where students use the Internet to access relevant and up-to-date information and then apply that knowledge through critical thinking by synthesizing information, analyzing content, and solving problems using creative thought.

OVERVIEW

A WebQuest is an educational tool used to engage students in the process of learning and to begin using real-world data and information found on the Internet. This Web-based activity can be an introductory or concluding activity, or it can be presented as an entire unit of study. WebQuests allow students to explore and discover information through important questions, investigation of resources, collaborative groups, role playing, and presentation.

As the teacher, you create an activity that uses quality resources that help answer the engaging "quest" that wraps your students into a role. For example, students can be literary critics, owners of a circus, a zoologist, or a politician running for office.

Once you identify a role for each student to play, resources are then provided to students. These resources have been prereviewed and evaluated by you to ensure the information is reliable and provides appropriate content to help students complete their WebQuest.

The students themselves are not responsible for going out onto the Internet to find quality resources. Rather, this is something you must accomplish and present to them at the start of the WebQuest activity. The main mission for your students is to investigate the task presented.

WebQuests are a perfect example of constructivist learning. As the teacher, you present a "big idea" question, and provide appropriate resources and instructional strategies so your students can explore and discover the information to answer important questions.

Rather than focusing on memorization of terms, terminology, or procedures, a structured WebQuest activity is designed to get students thinking critically about topics and content. The following sections depict how to design a quality WebQuest activity.

FORMATTING A WEBQUEST

Like any instructional activity, there is a structure and format to follow in order to ensure learning standards and objectives are being met, appropriate strategies are used, methods and tools are utilized, and appropriate feedback and assessments are given to ensure that students are learning what is intended.

The fundamental idea of a WebQuest is to provide an inquiry learning experience that allows students to:

• ask questions;
• make hypotheses;
• test hypotheses; and
• present new understanding to others.

Your goal as a teacher is to ensure that these experiences are taking place and are appropriate.

A WebQuest also provides opportunities for students to use a technology tool, such as the Internet, to research real-world up-to-date data and review current and relevant information to help solve real-world problems. Students can then take their collected data and place them into a spreadsheet to organize them and create a graph. They can also use a word processor to textually present their findings for others to read.

When students begin to think critically about a "big idea" question in the WebQuest task and begin using technology to analyze and evaluate information found, learning becomes meaningful and important. As the teacher and designer of the WebQuest, your task is to keep these central ideas in mind as you create the "quest."

Some areas to focus on include:

1. Standards and learning objectives;
2. Authentic activities and assessments;
3. Instructional strategies that encourage collaboration;
4. Opportunities for knowledge creation and exploration through discovery and exploration;
5. Resources that identify real-world data and relevant up-to-date information; and
6. Technology tools and resources to enhance your "big idea" question.

When designing a WebQuest, the Internet is a prominent resource for student investigation and discovery. The Internet provides an abundance of resources and data that are up to date, has primary sources readily available, and is accessible. Therefore, as a teacher creating a WebQuest, you should utilize relevant data and resources found online for your students to analyze and evaluate in order to solve the proposed problem.

In the design phase, you want to carefully plan the teaching and learning strategies, as well as the activities. Your responsibility is to identify quality resources and determine what you want your students to understand. What is the big picture? Remember the goal of a WebQuest is not to write a research paper, but instead explore and discover content and then share this new knowledge with others through a performance.

SECTIONS OF A WEBQUEST

There are six central sections to prepare when designing a WebQuest. Table 5.1 identifies each of these sections, as well as the Teacher's Page and Credits section. Within each section, you provide instructional strategies, quality resources, and investigative pointers in order to ensure that students collect and organize information appropriately, remain on task throughout the WebQuest, and learn and understand the material.

As in the development of any lesson, think about and provide instructional strategies that meet the needs of various student learning styles. Provide an

Table 5.1. WebQuest Design Sections

Section	Description
I. Introduction	• Introduce students to the activity. • Emphatically capture the students' attention. • Write from a student perspective. • Option to use an advanced organizer or overview to prepare students for what is to come. • Should be short in length.

II. Task	• Must be doable and interesting.
	• Task allows students to learn so that they will enhance their current knowledge and gather new understanding with others.
	• The "big idea" question is presented here.
	• Possible tasks include:
	  • Solving a problem
	  • Preparing and participating in a debate
	  • Designing a product or procedure
	  • Multimedia presentation
	  • Article to be written

III. Process	• Provide specific steps students should take to accomplish and complete the intended task. • Specific details on groups, roles, resources, and strategies are given. • Specific handouts students will use to complete each process are made available here. • This section is an ordered list, identifying the procedures that must be followed to ensure success in the WebQuest activity. • Be very specific and detailed.
IV. Evaluation	• A check sheet and/or rubric for students to review allows them to determine what is important to accomplish and understand in the WebQuest. • Identify whether the grade will be individual, group, or both.
V. Conclusion	• Provide closure to the WebQuest by providing a summary of what students accomplished and its relevancy to their overall learning. • Questions could also be posed for students to investigate further if they are interested. • This identifies learning as a continuous process.
VI. Resources	• Provide a list of resources that students can use to find necessary information. • Organize the information in categories so students can find appropriate information at a glance.
Teacher's Page	• This is the only section that is not written for the student. • Provide as much detail as possible about standards, objectives, and the WebQuest itself so another teacher can adopt your WebQuest or adapt it to his or her students.
Credits	• Provide a list of references and credits that were used in the WebQuest. • Remember to reference all images, music, recordings, and text.

overall structure of resources you have reviewed and approved so students stay on task to collect and organize information appropriately and learn and understand what is intended.

As you work through these various sections when designing your Web-Quest, remember this is an inquiry-oriented activity that is wrapped around a "big idea" question, learning standards, and objectives, and should provide an authentic task to engage students in exploring and creating their own understanding about a topic.

A WebQuest can be of varying length. It can be a single lesson or it can be one or two days of activity or even one to two months. The WebQuest should be presented in a Web page format. This is important so students can easily access Internet resources that you provide them.

For another view of how a WebQuest is assimilated, see Figure 5.1 below. This organizational chart provides a visual representation of a WebQuest, particularly how each section is integrated to tell a story and draw the learner into the WebQuest itself.

DESIGNING EACH SECTION OF YOUR WEBQUEST

Introduction

As with any well-constructed activity, you must first introduce the activity to the students. In the *Introduction* section of your WebQuest, capture student

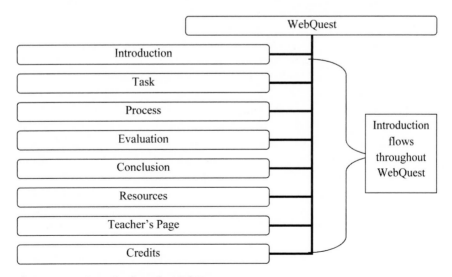

Figure 5.1. Organization of a WebQuest

attention to willingly participate in the WebQuest. Provide an inviting scenario that is both relevant and doable and assign roles or introduce resources that students can explore and investigate further.

Getting your students excited about participating in the WebQuest is simple if you focus on applying a scenario or activity that relates to their interest and experiences. For example, you can design a WebQuest so that students take a variety of roles, to include:

- A newspaper reporter investigating the story of Christopher Columbus and his quest for India and relating Columbus's experiences to other explorers past and present.
- A mathematician investigating census data collected during the Civil War to identify logistics and strategic movements of the generals and the battles fought, as well as how this information influenced conflicts past and present.
- A scientist investigating the life cycle of the animal kingdom and the likely outcome if an animal or plant is removed from the life cycle.

In each of the above examples, the WebQuest draws on the interests and experiences of the student and entices them to investigate a problem or an issue that is relevant to their personal lives and/or community. They are playing a role and the role revolves around why the learning objective is important.

This integration with prior knowledge and personal interest creates relevancy for the student and the activity itself. It also provides a connection for your students and builds on lessons learned in past activities to enhance learning in future activities.

In each example, a student should propose and test hypotheses, collect and analyze data, and then create new understanding by developing a presentation that can be viewed and shared with others. By taking on roles or scenarios, students are more likely to invest in the activity and have the expectation that something significant and important will occur when they reach the end of the WebQuest.

In the example of the scientist role, you could provide opportunities for your students to share their new understanding about a plant or animal taken out of the life cycle by having an evening poster session to present the data to parents and community members and allow for a question-and-answer period.

Students could prepare an article for the editorial section of the local newspaper to outline their findings and new understanding, and offer opportunities for the community to get more involved in life cycle issues of plants and animals from an environmental standpoint.

The *Introduction* does not have to stop at the first section of your Web-Quest. It can be embedded throughout the WebQuest to continually provide guidance and direction for your students. For example, an expert can provide commentary throughout the WebQuest to gain student attention and help provide feedback during the WebQuest. In the life cycle example, the expert can be a scientist from the Smithsonian or a parent who works at a research laboratory.

The *Introduction* section should provide specific details on what the WebQuest is about and what the expectations are. Its presentation should be concise so as not to overwhelm the students. Remember you want to encourage students to embark on this "quest" because it is important and then entice them to learn more and continue to the next section, the *Task*.

Below is an example of an introduction used to engage third graders studying past explorers. The focus of the lesson is for students to learn about the individual explorers as well as "the journey" or exploration itself.

Students will study the exploration of the Americas by:

* *Describing the accomplishments of Christopher Columbus, Juan Ponce de Léon, Jacques Cartier, and Christopher Newport;*
* *Identifying reasons for exploring, the information gained, and the results from the travels.*

Introduction

Ahoy!

Early explorers needed a lot of skills to investigate territories that were unknown and unfamiliar to them. Explorers encountered unfamiliar animals, languages, customs, foods, terrain, climates, and illnesses.

Just as the early explorers discovered new worlds so others could learn more about the world outside of their community, so will you. Through this exploration, you will investigate the new world's environment, people, and characteristics. There is a local explorer looking for a recorder. Are you interested in the position?

If so, go to the next section of the WebQuest, the Task, to begin this voyage.

Figure 5.2 Introduction Example

The *Introduction* shown above is specific, engaging, and provides a relevant reason for students to continue to the next section. Students have been introduced to both time and place as well as what their expectations will be. They are engaged and ready to go. It is a great start.

Task

The next section of a WebQuest is the *Task*. First and foremost, the question for you in this section is: *What specifically do you want your students to do and accomplish?*

Secondarily, you want to consider how you can make the WebQuest meaningful to your students personally in terms of their community, lifestyle, and/ or interests.

Remember the "big idea" question introduced above? In this section, you want to spell it out for your students and make sure that you grab their attention. This question must be designed so that it will encourage students to think and explore the topic in depth and at a deeper level.

The idea of the *Task* is for students to explore the "big idea" question by investigating the resources you provided. At the same time, students are expected to pull in past information and relate this new information to an authentic context, their lives, and the world at large.

Within the *Task*, you also provide specific expectations that you want students to perform in order to complete the WebQuest. In order to do this, provide a brief description of what you want your students to accomplish throughout the WebQuest. Explain what performances they are expected to complete by the end of the WebQuest.

With each section, you are building your WebQuest and slowly engaging your students into the process of working on the problem or issue you outlined. You will go into further detail in the next section, the *Process*. Remember, each section of the WebQuest builds on the next section and slowly pulls the students deeper into the "quest" itself. Designing a WebQuest is like telling a story with the final pages of the book missing.

It is during the development of the *Task* section that you find all the resources to help your students best complete the WebQuest. Once you have resources that provide interesting and quizzical paths for students to explore, then it is time to begin developing the WebQuest itself. Finding the resources first helps keep the WebQuest relevant and aligned with your standards and the overall goal of the activity.

As you create the *Task* section of your WebQuest, be sure to include appropriate scaffolding for your students. This helps make the tasks manageable and doable. It also encourages them to begin the process of thinking about

Task

You have just been hired by an explorer to help investigate and report on a new world. The questions that you will explore and investigate are not easy so you will need to work in groups as you set sail on a journey across the vast ocean for the exploration.

This trip will be filled with new adventures! The explorer of this voyage needs a good reporter to keep the Ship's Exploration Journal in order to record all findings and discoveries, to include, people, places, cultures, foods, artifacts, and the voyage itself.

Your group will also design an Exhibit, using your Exploration Journal as a resource, to inform the community about far away discoveries on your return and how these discoveries have impacted our lives today.

You will be divided into four different explorer groups. Each group will be assigned an explorer that will be Captain of the Ship.

The explorers are:

• Christopher Columbus,
• Juan Ponce de Leon,
• Jacques Cartier, and
• Christopher Newport.

As the reporter, you will be in charge of the Ship's Exploration Journal and the collection of all artifacts in order to share the journey and the discoveries with others. Requirements are provided below.

In your investigation you will:

• Observe the strength of mind of the explorer,
• Document all trials and tribulations during the journey,
• List discoveries and achievements, and
• Reflect on the importance of discovery and achievement in today's world.

In addition, you will note:

• New cultures, languages, customs, and products,
• Any problems encountered, and
• Interesting facts that were discovered.

Figure 5.3. Task Example

The Exploration Journal will be used to take notes and collect artifacts during the exploration itself. The Journal must contain the following items:

- Reason for exploration,
- Biographical information of the explorer,
- Personality of the explorer,
- Cargo and food report with images, sketches, position on ship, etc.,
- Sketches or images of encounters, such as, boats, maps, people, jewelry, foods, plants, animals, structures, etc. that were encountered and collected during the voyage, and
- Navigator report.

Your Exploration Group will design an Exhibit in the appropriate theme of the new world explored, highlighting the information collected during your travels.

The Exhibit participants will be your peers, parents, and the school community.

This Exhibit can use PowerPoint, HyperStudio, images, sound clips, poster, or/ and brochure to display information and content found.

Figure 5.3. (*continued*)

the content, the goals of the activity, the expectations, and their role in the WebQuest itself.

This can be accomplished in outline form. The goal of providing scaffolding is to ensure that a connection to prior learning is included. It also helps students develop a schema, e.g., a pattern that is continuously called upon and reformatted when students encounter the same topics and inquiry skills in future activities.

Process

The *Process* section provides specific details about the group roles in the WebQuest as well as each individual group member's role. As suggested earlier, a WebQuest should have collaboration among students built into the WebQuest, whereby each member in the group assumes a different role or perspective.

In this section, you want to outline the following specific attributes:

- Outline the goals of the WebQuest;
- Restate your interesting and engaging problem for students to explore and discover;

Process

Now let's begin our Exploration!

You and your group will be in charge of the Exploration Journal. The Exploration Journal will contain many different artifacts and written accounts of the journey itself. You will use your Journal to design and create your Exhibit.

You will be divided into groups that will investigate and go along on the exploration. Your group will be members of the crew of one of the explorers below:

- Christopher Columbus
- Juan Ponce de Leon
- Jacques Cartier, or
- Christopher Newport

Your teacher will give you your Ship's assignment before you begin. Through this exploration, you will collect information and be prepared as a group to share this new information with the class in an exhibit.

- Why Explore?

    In order to do a good job for your Captain, you must understand who he or she is. You will start by watching a short video about explorations. (Video link).

    Use your Exploration Journal to list factual information about exploring that you discovered while watching the video.

    Take notes on what explorations consist of.

    Next, what makes a good explorer?

    After writing and reflecting in your Journal, we will discuss your findings as a class. During this discussion, we will identify similarities and differences of explorers and identify some key characteristics of a good explorer. During this discussion, do not forget to jot down some interesting facts in your Journal!

    Now it is time to explore a couple of Web sites to learn some interesting facts about your specific explorer.

    Resources

    - Why Explore?

        http://library.thinkquest.org/C001692/english/index.php3?subject=why

Figure 5.4. Process Example

- Get to know your explorer.

  It is important before we begin any exploration to learn about your Captain, the explorer. Who is this person? Who commissioned him or her? Why is this Commission important? What do you think the personality of the explorer is?

  Resources:

  - Enchanted Learning: Juan Ponce de Leon

    http://www.enchantedlearning.com/explorers/page/d/deleon.shtml

  - Encarta: Juan Ponce de Leon

    http://encarta.msn.com/ ponce_de_leon.html

  - History Channel: Juan Ponce de Leon

    http://www.history.com/encyclopedia.do?articleId=219594

- Cargo and Food Report

  As you set sail on your exploration, you must make sure that your ship's cargo list is complete. You want to make sure that the ship is fully stocked with food for your crew for this long and uncertain voyage.

  Gather information about foods that were available during the time period of your explorer and design a list of items you will need for your ship.

  Make sure you address such questions as:

  - What will the crew drink?
  - What types of fruits, vegetables, and meats will make the journey?
  - Will flour be needed?
  - What herbs can be used to make food tasty?
  - How will food be stored?
  - Will you stop along the way to get more food?
  - Will you have opportunities to fish or hunt for food?
  - What else will you bring on your voyage? Investigate what else your explorer might have brought with him by thinking about what kind of clothes were needed, what tools were needed, trading trinkets or other items you discover.

  When you have your ship's Cargo and Food Report, add it to your Exploration Journal.

Figure 5.4. *(continued)*

Resources

Juan Ponce de Leon

- World Fact Book

  http://www.faqs.org/docs/factbook/countrylisting.html

- Navigator Report

  Now that you are familiar with your explorer and your ship is fully stocked, it is time to set sail. But how will the Captain know where to go? Well, as his or her first mate that is your job to make sure the Captain is able to reach his destination.

  - First, you will determine how explorers navigated their ships during this time period and report your findings so that the Captain can be prepared when you set sail.

  - Second, you will design and create a map of the journey the explorer took to reach his or her destination. You will need to print out a world map that shows where your explorer began and the route he or she took to reach the final destination. (World Map Worksheet). Make sure that you label your map with the following information:

    - Country where the explorer started his or her voyage

    - Country where the voyage ended

    - The body of water traveled across

    - The equator and different hemispheres

  - Draw a navigational symbol showing North, South, East, and West

Resources

Juan Ponce de Leon

- Encarta: Ponce de Leon exploration map

  http://encarta.msn.com/media_461517666/Early_European _Explorers.html

Finally, draw a picture of the ship and what it must have looked like when the crew landed at their destination. Don't forget to take note of such things as wildlife or rivers in your drawing.

Add all these items to your Exploration Journal.

- Achievements of Explorer Report

Land Ahoy!

You have safely made it to your destination!

Now as the first mate it is your responsibility to continue to write notes in your Explorer's Journal in order to keep an accurate and up-to-date report for everyone in your homeland. Make sure to log, in your Exploration Journal, information that will be relevant for your Exhibit, such as:

- Where did you land?

- What was found?

- Were there any native people? If so, who were they? What was interesting about them? What was similar? Identify who they were and what they were like.

- Are there raw materials to build homes or survive? What kind of homes might you build?

- What types of plants were there to eat? Should seeds be sent over on future voyages? If so, what types of seed would be best for the climate and terrain?

- What kind of wildlife was there?

- Is this the final destination of the explorer or does the explorer set sail soon afterwards and explore further?

Everyone at home is very curious, so your Exploration Journal must be very detailed. It should tell of your adventure and the discovery of this new land and what it has to offer.

Don't forget to include in your Exploration Journal at least two drawings of interesting artifacts so everyone at home can see what this new land and people look like.

Resources

Juan Ponce de Leon

- Social Studies for Kids: Juan Ponce de Leon

    http://www.socialstudiesforkids.com/articles/worldhistory/juanponcedeleon1.htm

*Note: this Process is only a fragment of the Process section as only limited resources and information were provided to this illustration. In your actual Process section, more relevant and useful resources and text would need to be provided so students do not have to struggle to find information. Be specific with your resources.

Figure 5.4. (*continued*)

- Provide quality and relevant resources to help students explore the problem in detail; and
- Assign meaningful collaborative groups to help students identify a specific role or perspective of the problem.

All of these attributes provide the WebQuest with a sense of relevancy and meaningful real-world experience that will aid in attracting your students' attention and pulling them into the WebQuest.

The goal of the WebQuest is to create an activity that will engage students in the topic and content to be explored so that they can discover new information and go beyond current knowledge to develop their own understanding and then present this new understanding to others in a meaningful way. The *Process* section identifies and describes strategies and resources you want your students to use to complete the *Task*.

Evaluation

In an inquiry-oriented activity such as a WebQuest, students should be aware from the beginning how they are going to be evaluated. What are the expectations of this WebQuest and what is important for them to understand? To do this, design a rubric that identifies your learning objectives and is easy for your students to follow and comprehend.

You may want to highlight Bloom's Taxonomy of application, synthesis, and evaluation to ensure that students are thinking critically about the task at hand. An authentic evaluation tool such as a rubric is the best method to use with a WebQuest.

When students review the rubric below they are able to determine what is expected of them throughout the WebQuest activity. There are specific criteria required for success. The student will see that the value 4 is the highest score, but it also allows students to go beyond by adding a value of 5 if they demonstrate exceptionally outstanding effort.

The rubric also allows group members to evaluate each other. The following is an example of a complete and well-rounded rubric that will keep students on task and focused throughout the WebQuest. The most important thing about using a rubric as an evaluation and assessment tool is that it be relevant, consistent, and fair.

Conclusion

The conclusion of a WebQuest provides a summary of the activity, a congratulations to your students for completing the WebQuest, and questions for further investigation.

Table 5.2. Evaluation Example

Category	Above and Beyond 5	Exemplary 4	Accomplished 3	Developing 2	Beginning 1	Score
What did you learn about your explorer and the exploration itself?	Identified and listed more than 7 findings and artifacts. Wrote more than 4 sentences without errors and with excellent sentence structure.	Identified and listed 7 or more findings and artifacts. Wrote 4 or more sentences without errors, and with excellent sentence structure.	Identified and listed 4 or more findings and artifacts. Wrote sentences with good sentences structure and few errors.	Identified and listed 3 or 4 findings and artifacts. Wrote 2-3 sentences with several errors.	Identified and listed 2 or 3 findings and artifacts. Wrote 1-2 sentences without sentence structure.	
Completed task for exploration.	Completed each step within the process and gathered evidence. No grammatical errors.	Completed all areas without grammatical errors.	Completed 4-5 areas with few grammatical errors.	Completed 3-4 areas with several grammatical errors.	Completed 2 areas with many grammatical errors.	
Ecosystem Scavenger hunt.	Identified all 7 aspects and was able to explain why each was important to another part of the ecosystem.	Found all 7 aspects and could explain why each was important to the ecosystem.	Found 5 to 7 aspects and could explain why several were important to the ecosystem.	Found 3 to 5 aspects and could explain why a couple were important to the ecosystem.	Found 1 to 3 aspects and could not articulate why any were important to the ecosystem.	

Category					
Diagram of your type of farm.	Achieved exemplary level, then included ideas to enhance the farming experience.	Detailed drawing of farm includes all aspects of farm ecosystem. Color and extras added.	Drawing of farm with 3 or more aspects of farm ecosystem. Color and an extra added.	Drawing of farm. May include aspect of ecosystem. May include color, but limited effort.	Drawing of farm. Does not include aspect of ecosystem. Little color, little effort.
Commercial	Achieved exemplary level and included props, costumes etc.	Included an identifiable jingle, humor, and many aspects learned about the type of farm. Outstanding effort.	Included jingle, some humor, and several aspects about the type of farm. Could engage audience more.	Included jingle, little humor, and one or two aspects about the farm style. Lacks enthusiasm.	May include jingle and little humor. May include aspects about farm. Minimal effort.

Conclusion

> Your explorer cannot thank you enough for all your attention to detail in the Ship's Exploration Journal. The King and Queen also thank you for the detail letter and drawings of the newly discovered land.
>
> It is time to share your Exploration Journal with your classmates!
>
> What does it mean when you say that someone is an explorer? How do explorations impact other's lives? Are there any present day explorers?

Figure 5.5. Conclusion Example

Resources

In the Resources section, provide a list of all resources students will use to complete the WebQuest task. This list should be easily accessible and readable. These same resources are also in the Process section of your WebQuest.

The reason you also place them in this section is for easy access. It helps to eliminate student confusion or frustration while completing the WebQuest activity. This way students remain focused on achieving the goal of the lesson.

The resources that you use for your WebQuest will primarily come from the Internet. You can use a variety of resources as long as they are relevant. Resources can include video, sound files, maps, experts, graphics, manipulatives, models, and images. Any resource can be used that allows students to think about each element within their task and motivates them to continue with the WebQuest.

Resources

Juan Ponce de Leon

- Enchanted Learning: Juan Ponce de Leon

    http://www.enchantedlearning.com/explorers/page/d/deleon.shtml

- Encarta: Juan Ponce de Leon

    http://encarta.msn.com/ ponce_de_leon.html

- History Channel: Juan Ponce de Leon

    http://www.history.com/encyclopedia.do?articleId=219594

Figure 5.6. Resources Example

Teacher's Page

In this section, provide information for other teachers who may be interested in adopting your WebQuest. Provide all the information needed to implement the activity successfully. Standards of learning and technology standards covered should be clearly identified.

Also, provide your "big idea" question, resources that you utilized throughout your WebQuest, and teaching strategies implemented. In addition, identify any problems that a teacher may encounter with a specific resource or strategy.

You may also want to identify any supplies or resources that are necessary to complete the WebQuest. It is also helpful to include a note regarding any changes made since your last revision (if applicable) or ideas for extensions with specific students. You may additionally request that teachers who have used your WebQuest contact you regarding what worked best and what could be improved upon. The more detailed you are on the *Teacher's Page* the better.

A sampling of scaffolding activities that teachers may implement to prepare students for the WebQuest should also be provided. Outline each activity that the groups work through to complete the WebQuest. The most important focus of this section is to prepare prospective users of your WebQuest before

Teacher's Page

- Background of WebQuest

- Standards of Learning (SOLs)
  - Content
  - Technology

- Notes and important information about the WebQuest

- Teaching strategies and methods

- Resources used

- Possible resources to add to the WebQuest

- Further reading about the topic

- Contact me (Feedback)

Figure 5.7. Teacher's Page Example

Credits

Images on page one retrieved from...

Content for ____ retrieved from....

Etc.

Figure 5.8. Credits Example

they begin implementing the WebQuest with their students in their class-rooms. What do you want them to know?

You can provide links to relevant pages of your WebQuest to help teachers see and review what your expectations are for the WebQuest. Remember, this is an interactive Web document, so using hyperlinks to areas within your WebQuest is very appropriate and useful.

Credits

Make sure to formally cite all sources used in your WebQuest in the *Credits* section. This includes images, video, and text. Citing sources is important to model good Internet behavior to your students. In this section, you also want to list all resources used throughout your WebQuest to provide easy access to your students.

As discussed above, you can create a WebQuest that is engaging, interesting, and fun, and at the same time provide opportunities for students to explore and discover information and then present this new information to a larger audience. As illustrated, this is not a static research project or an activity to have students memorize terms and terminology. The following WebQuest Template can also serve as a guide to help get you started.

CHAPTER SUMMARY

In a WebQuest, students work in collaborative groups on a relevant topic that aligns with your learning standards and, at the same time, are encouraged to further explore the material in more detail.

WebQuest Template

Title of the Lesson

A WebQuest for xth Grade for Content Area

Designed by _____

Contact Information _____

Graphic that highlights task, content, or subject

Introduction | Task | Process | Evaluation | Conclusion | Resources | Teacher's Page | Credits

Introduction

Introduce the students to the activity and emphatically capture the students' attention. Prepare your WebQuest with your students in mind. Use an advanced organizer or overview to prepare the student for what is to come. The introduction should be short in length.

Task

Must be doable and interesting and allow students to advance their understanding of the information they have gathered in order to share their newly acquired information with others. This is where you place your "big idea" question. Some possible tasks could include:

- Solve a problem

- Prepare and participate in a debate

- Design a product or procedure

- Multimedia presentation

- Article to be written

Process

Provide specific steps that students will take and accomplish to complete the intended task. Specific details on groups, roles, resources, and strategies are given. Specific handouts that students use to complete each process are provided. This section is organized in an ordered list, identifying the procedures

Figure 5.9.   WebQuest Template

that must be followed to ensure success in the WebQuest. Make certain that your presentation is very specific and detailed.

Evaluation

Provide a check sheet and/or rubric for students to review in order to determine what is important for them to accomplish and understand in the WebQuest. Identify whether their grade will be individual, group, or both.

Conclusion

Provide closure to the WebQuest by providing a summary of what students accomplished and its relevancy to their overall learning. You could also pose questions for students to investigate further. This identifies learning as a continuous process.

Resources

A list of resources should be provided that students can review to find information. The resources should be organized into categories so that the information is easy to access.

Teacher's Page

Provide as much detail as possible about standards, objectives, and the WebQuest itself so that another teacher can adopt your WebQuest.

Credits

Provide a list of references and credits that were used in your WebQuest. Reference all images, music, recordings, and text. Also, if you used other resources such as books or people, you would list them in this section.

Figure 5.9. (*continued*)

The design of your WebQuest is very important. Since this is a WebQuest that will be located on the Web, you want to think about interactivity, graphics and fonts used, as well as your use of colors to help engage students.

Overall, a WebQuest provides information. Students think critically about this information and then present it to others as a group. As a teacher, your goal is to provide quality information and effective learning strategies in order to get students thinking about and creating new knowledge. Students should not passively work through your WebQuest. Instead, they should be talking, debating, discussing, sharing, analyzing, and critiquing information and ideas.

CHAPTER REFLECTION

1. Summarize three main goals of a WebQuest.
2. What makes a WebQuest an inquiry-oriented activity?
3. Why is it important for the "big idea" question to drive a WebQuest?
4. When designing a WebQuest, it is best to provide relevant and quality resources for students to use. Explain why this is so important.

SKILL-BUILDING ACTIVITY

Throughout this chapter, we explored how to create a WebQuest using the Internet. The focus was on engaging your students in an interesting and do-able activity so that they were motivated to think, explore, and discover new information. Your goal is to create a WebQuest that aligns with your learning standards, is developed around an interesting and doable "big idea" question, uses quality resources, and provides opportunities for students to complete a meaningful presentation of their new knowledge.

Chapter Six

Creating a Web Inquiry Activity

A Web inquiry activity uses the unfiltered Web to encourage students to explore and investigate information. Raw resources, such as primary-source documents, book reviews, and data, are accessed by students so they can ask questions, explore content, and determine possible results. One reason why Web inquiry is beneficial from an educational standpoint is the opportunity for questions to be tied both to standards of learning and real-life events, problems, resources, and data.

As Bloom's Taxonomy suggests, teachers should move their students from memorization to higher-level investigation and thinking. This is done by creating activities that provide opportunities for students to synthesize and analyze information in order for them to begin thinking critically about questions posed in all situations. From there, they can then develop questions on their own. Ideally it is best if students can do this with unfiltered information to provide a real-world approach to learning.

OVERVIEW

A Web inquiry activity revolves around good open-ended questions tied to learning standards. When you have learning standards that highlight inquiry, you can begin writing your objectives. How do you want students to demonstrate their understanding of these standards and what will your students produce when they complete the activity?

Because this is a Web inquiry activity, good online data are required. Students find data that use real-time databases or primary-source documents and then they are able to utilize this timely, meaningful, and raw data to help answer questions. This allows students to explore an open-ended question that you provided to them in an unfiltered way. In other words, no one has interpreted these data for them, like a textbook author. When students look at raw data they must critically think about information to find possible solutions.

The purpose of a Web inquiry activity is to provide students with meaningful opportunities to use raw data, e.g., data that have not be filtered, so they can both manipulate and interpret them to create meaning and sift through and discover possible solutions.

For example, students can explore global warming on many different levels. Working in collaborative groups, they can explore specific elements of this broad issue. In one group, for instance, students can investigate a question about alternative energy sources, both the benefits and shortcomings.

A sample database that students can draw data from could be the commodity stock exchange for live data. Questions could be posed, such as:

- How has the price of corn changed over the past five years?
- What are some of the benefits of this price change?
- What are some of the drawbacks of this price change?
- How do these changes impact the environment?

A Web inquiry activity is similar to a WebQuest because it uses information primarily from the Web, except a WebQuest contains resources for students to explore chosen by you, the teacher.

A Web inquiry activity is designed to give guidance to the teacher but not necessarily the student. Rather, this is true scientific inquiry such that the inquiry activity provides little information and guidance in order for the student to investigate, discover, and ultimately make predictions. Maximum flexibility is given to students to encourage creativity in completing a Web inquiry activity.

The only part of a Web inquiry activity that you provide to your students is the first section, the part called the *Hook*. As stated earlier, the idea is to provide as little information as possible to your students in order to enhance the inquiry elements and overall creative thinking of the activity itself.

In this process, it is important that in your role as the teacher, you guide your students throughout the inquiry activity. You ask questions and direct students to appropriate resources that will help them find answers to critical questions.

INQUIRY USING THE INTERNET

The best Web inquiry activities start with an open-ended question. Open-ended questions do not identify a solution. Thus, students are compelled to explore many possibilities or hypotheses in order to solve the overall problem.

For example, in a science unit where the theme is global warming, the open-ended question could focus on how human consumption and production impacts the rising global climate. Students use prior understanding of climate, consumption, and production and then begin identifying what information they need to best answer this question.

Students begin researching a variety of data sources such as weather data, government records and reports, and production rates of goods and services. Students then take this new information and combine it in a white paper that they submit to local community leaders.

Web inquiry activities provide valid and reliable Web resources that give students opportunities to collect and discover information. For example, raw data sites such as the U.S. Census Bureau at http://www.census.gov/schools/facts allows students to collect data over time for population growth in specific parts of the country. This helps answer questions about the possibilities of global warming as it relates to population growth in urban and rural areas.

A Web inquiry activity is focused on either guided or open inquiry. In *guided* inquiry, the teacher guides the process of student inquiry, either by providing resources or by asking leading questions. A guided inquiry could be used to introduce students to the process of inquiry. This is not a natural skill. All of us must be taught how to develop questions, answer questions, create hypotheses, and make predictions. How do we look critically at information to make good decisions?

Utilizing *open* inquiry, open-ended questions are posed by the teacher to students. Instead of guiding the discovery process of the student, the teacher facilitates the process and allows students to take the lead role in the discovery and investigative process. The teacher therefore assists the inquiry process to ensure that students are on task, productive, and learning what is important and intended.

Regardless of which inquiry method you choose, guided or open, an inquiry activity has the potential to provide an authentic learning experience to your students. Students then are able to practice critical thinking in order to build the Web inquiry activity around an authentic problem.

This elicits student interest in the topic and helps them discover relevancy to the content itself. How many times have you heard, "Why do I need to know this?"? Through this authentic Web inquiry activity, questions such as this are readily answered.

Guidelines in any class activity are important and this is no exception when it comes to a Web inquiry-oriented activity. Whether you are using guided or open inquiry, the need for guidelines applies. Your students need structure or they will get lost throughout the process. If this happens, learning the intended objectives will not occur. When designing a Web inquiry activity, you must include structure into the activity itself.

Traditional inquiry activities have revolved around set answers or solutions. Students typically practiced inquiry skills, but each completed activity had a specific answer. Resources provided and used by students came primarily through textbooks. Even science experiments oftentimes had prescribed outcomes.

As educators involved in 21st-century teaching and learning, we now have the potential to have students access live information found on the Internet. They can manipulate raw (and real) data to question information and tie this new knowledge into their own understanding. In order for this to happen effectively, as the teacher you must pose good questions, use relevant and timely resources, and ultimately encourage students to build inquiry skills.

A Web inquiry activity is both a hands-on and minds-on activity from the perspective of both the teacher and the students. As the teacher, you must actively participate in the activity with your students by asking questions and guiding them through the inquiry process. This active participation from you provides students with continued opportunities to test their theories and assumptions in order to answer needed questions.

For students to be successfully engaged, the teacher must provide a variety of learning strategies such as visual mind maps, small and large collaborative groups, think-pair-share, and opportunities for discussion, reflection, and feedback. Each strategy will help students scaffold new understanding.

One major benefit of a Web inquiry activity is the constant connection you have with your students to ensure that good questions are being asked and answered. If you want your students to sit quietly at a computer and work solo on an activity, a Web inquiry activity is not the activity of choice. A Web inquiry activity is an interactive exercise.

WHY WEB INQUIRY?

The Internet provides its users with many different sources of information. This information comes in the form of primary-source documents and raw data, such as research statistics, news articles, journals, blogs, wikis, images, and video. Each source provides an opportunity for students to gather resources and then to manipulate the information to answer important questions and create new meaning.

Data obtained from the Internet are both quantitative and qualitative in nature. They may be created and posted by various news organizations, developed as personal reflections and opinions, or support raw facts and figures developed and maintained by governments and other public or private organizations.

This use of unfiltered information found on the Web allows students the opportunity to organize and decipher resources to aid in answering important questions. For example, this is how an economist makes decisions in his or her daily profession, e.g., by analyzing raw data and then manipulating and synthesizing them in order to answer specific questions.

This process is a good example of thinking critically about topics that are relevant to us, both inside and outside the classroom. A student could study economics by reading the textbook and learn about the gross national product or the consumer price index.

But these key economic indicators can also come to life by accessing the Department of Labor's (DOL) Web site at http://www.dol.gov/dol/audience/ aud-students.htm to find actual data that DOL economists are reviewing to make decisions. This real-world application helps to create meaning and validity for students and they are better able to grasp how both of these concepts impact the nation's economy.

This real-world approach provides a different learning experience for students than just the textbook alone. When you are using the Internet as a resource through either guided or open inquiry, your students have opportunities to experience and discover knowledge. This is a very powerful learning opportunity.

When the Internet was initially introduced into K–12 schools, it was used as a traditional research tool. Instead of students going to the library, searching the card catalog, and choosing a book from the shelf, they were sent to a search engine, such as Google, where they typed in random key words and hopefully found useful information that could be included in a report. This type of Internet research does not allow for deep discovery or investigation.

A true Web inquiry project is achieved by asking questions and then critically evaluating resources to determine if they are accurate, credible, and can help solve the overall problem. As new resources are found, more questions are asked. The benefit of the Internet in this process is online databases. Online databases are unfiltered and contain raw data from government Web sites as well as primary-source documents, often found housed at universities.

How is Web inquiry different from using a textbook or a book from the library? How is it different from a simple Google search? The difference is raw unfiltered data. Using raw data provides students with full and complete information, thereby allowing them to ask questions and determine for themselves the best possible answers to a problem.

Instead of having the answer interpreted from someone else and then presented to your students, they now additionally have the opportunity to use the Internet to discover and explore information and create their own interpretations, connections, and meanings. At the same time, students are learning important research skills through finding, accessing, and synthesizing the real-world data.

For example, suppose you had a social studies unit that revolved around students learning about U.S. presidents and their role in United States history. Students could read the textbook about each president's role, but how much richer the experience and new knowledge gained if students were able to access the American Memory Project at the Library of Congress.

At this Web site, http://memory.loc.gov, students are able to explore primary-source documents for the various presidents, such as letters from Thomas Jefferson and Abraham Lincoln. They learn not only about presidential policies, but also past presidents' feelings and intentions.

The open-ended question could therefore center on asking students: *Why did U.S. presidents make the decisions that they did and how have their actions impacted the United States and the world at large?*

In today's "flat world," it is important to provide opportunities for students to *think.* We need to move away from transcribing, summarizing, and reformatting collected information toward using information to make decisions, ask questions, create, and present new knowledge in meaningful ways for others to learn from and explore.

WHAT IS WEB INQUIRY?

A Web inquiry activity is a strategy for incorporating the Internet into your curriculum so students are engaged. It provides structure and specific guidelines to ensure that teachers stay focused on student learning and discovery. At the same time, it teaches students good inquiry skills, such as questioning and finding information to make informed decisions.

A Web inquiry activity provides a student-centered approach. It gives students the opportunity to take the lead in their learning process as well as contains elements of constructivism where students can construct their own meaning.

Although Web inquiry activities are designed to provide more control to your students, the teacher still plays an active role by facilitating and guiding the learning process. You do this by scaffolding activities to ensure that students are on task and are asking good questions, finding relevant resources, and developing creative insights about the topics being explored.

For example, when studying the Civil War, why not have students understand not just about the conflict, but also the personal stories and experiences of people who lived during that time and the impact of the war among families, neighbors, and communities? Studying the Civil War could include accessing primary-source documents via the Web, such as from the Library of Congress, of letters from soldiers to their family members. This would help to answer an open-ended and "big idea" question, such as: *How did the Civil War impact families and communities?*

Census data obtained during that time period could also be accessed to determine who lived in these communities. Newspaper articles could be retrieved to determine the news of the cities and towns during that time period. Each would provide information and allow students to identify answers to their questions about this time in history and how the Civil War truly impacted the United States.

PLANNING FOR INQUIRY

When planning a Web inquiry activity, consider the following elements:

1. Identify an open-ended question to pose to students that aligns with your learning standards and objectives.
2. Identify Internet resources that provide students with the most complete way to answer the posed question. Try to find raw data, primary sources, and library databases.
3. Identify learning strategies students can use to manipulate the data to best answer the posed question. Small-group work, using a spreadsheet to organize, compute, and display data, or interviewing community members to collect primary data are some examples.
4. Identify possible answers to the open-ended question using a variety of sources and then present this new information to others using the Internet, presentation software, or multimedia.

As demonstrated in the above list, a clear and defined plan is needed to guide students down the path of inquiry. Lessons must be well defined or the intended goal of the lesson will be lost. You want to create an activity that piques curiosity, engages their creative mindset, and encourages them to investigate further.

As you identify important open-ended questions to help focus your activity, the next step is to determine the process of inquiry that you want your students to take. Throughout these steps, you want students to reflect on the

Figure 6.1. Web Inquiry Activity Process

information gathered and how this new information helps or hinders solving the proposed problem.

During this inquiry process, students reflect on the proposed question and then begin to ask questions, identify procedures to help answer the proposed question, gather and investigate figures, analyze and manipulate data, and then present their findings for others to use and learn from. Figure 6.1 identifies the process students should follow during a Web inquiry activity.

DESIGNING A WEB INQUIRY ACTIVITY

As discussed earlier in the chapter, the main idea of a Web inquiry activity is for students to work with and manipulate information to create new understandings. Within this activity, teachers are not giving material to students, rather they are providing a structured opportunity for students to work with all types of evidence such as numbers, text, images, sounds, video, etc. This real-world access to knowledge allows students to think, question, and explore.

A Web inquiry activity serves as a learning tool, but even once you have identified a good open-ended question and provided a variety of data types, you must still identify and align both with your learning goal. What is important for your students to understand about the topic? Below are four specific questions to help organize your thoughts around designing a good inquiry activity:

1. Why is this problem important and how does it relate to the real world?
2. What specific tools and information are needed and what is the best way to collect this new knowledge?
3. What do you want students to understand?
4. How can this new knowledge be presented so others can learn from it?

When designing a Web inquiry activity, think about and then plan for what is important for students to understand. Create an open-ended question that aligns with your learning objectives and engages your students to remain on task. One way to do this is to break down your learning goal into questions that you design your activity around, such as the four questions shown above.

As introduced earlier in the chapter, a Web inquiry activity is different from a WebQuest. In a WebQuest, you are creating a structured inquiry-oriented activity that provides Web resources at specific points throughout the WebQuest to help students complete the task. Students are assigned specific roles that provide them with a real-world problem. They are also given outlined procedures to follow in order to complete the task effectively and efficiently.

It is possible for a WebQuest to be completed independently by the student because the "quest" itself is organized throughout with resources, a specific task, and well-identified procedures that provide scaffolding throughout the process.

A Web inquiry activity is intended to be a guided discovery, with the teacher being directly involved in order to scaffold the student throughout the process of investigation. While the teacher plays a central role, a Web inquiry activity is intended to be completed in small groups.

THE WEB INQUIRY DEVELOPMENT PROCESS

This section provides an overview of the six parts to be considered when designing a Web inquiry activity:

1. The *Hook* that grabs the students' attention.
2. Getting students to identify other questions.

Table 6.1. Organizing Your Web Inquiry Activity

Questions for the Web Inquiry:	How to Accomplish:
• Why is this problem important and how does it relate to the real world?	Impact: Geography, Anthropology, and Sociology. Problem Statement: An organization is relocating employees to another region of the world. Real World: Employees must know the culture and environment in order to best prepare for this relocation.
• What specific tools and information are needed and what is the best way to collect this new knowledge?	Type: Map of region and information on place in the world. Explore Web sites to gather data about culture, weather, and topography: • Google Earth • CIA Fact Book • United Nations Students utilize facts, figures, pictures, video clips, personal Web sites, country Web sites, Government Web sites, etc.
• What do you want students to understand?	Differences and similarities in culture, customs, language, and geographic environment.
• How can this new knowledge be presented so others can learn from it?	Present information: Using presentation software, students develop a brochure to provide important facts about laws, culture, customs, environment, and language of the country being relocated into.

Activity:

Working in small, collaborative groups, students gather information about Denmark, a European country where a U.S. firm is expanding into and sending expatriates. Students use various Web tools to discover the country's customs, environment, industries, foods, language, and culture in order to provide a guide to employees that are transferring to the country.

Evaluation:

A rubric that includes criteria that cover the quality of data identified and how the data help solve the problem. The rubric will also provide a criterion on presentation effectiveness.

Time frame to complete: Two 50 minute class periods.

3. Procedures to guide students through the process of inquiry.
4. Exploration of data.
5. Analyzing data.
6. Presenting findings.

The Hook

This is the only section that your students see. The *Hook* is the open-ended, "big idea" question that grabs students' attention and takes them into the problem to be explored and discovered. This is where you provide a topical question. Students take this question and as a group begin identifying sub-questions. The topical question engages the students in the task and most importantly sparks their interest.

In this section, you want students to identify key areas within the topical question and begin reflecting on the question. Completed as a class, this allows students to identify prior knowledge and highlight key and important points to focus on during the process of inquiry.

Your role as the teacher during the *Hook* stage is to:

- encourage students to reflect on prior knowledge;
- interest them in new material to be presented;
- provide the *Hook* (e.g., the open-ended question);
- provide supporting ideas and resources for the initial *Hook* question; and
- have students start moving forward with the activity.

As stated earlier, the *Hook* should grab students' attention to begin their investigation. It is important that the question be relevant to your curriculum and tie into student interests. It must be engaging, structured, and open-ended. Since this is the only part of the activity that students see, try to make it good.

Other Questions

As students become pulled into the initial question that you provided them, their interest in the activity grows and they become "hooked." As the teacher, your role is to provide students with opportunities to draw on prior knowledge and encourage them to begin asking deeper questions of your topical question. From there, they can begin making predictions about the topic being explored.

Different strategies can be used to begin the inquiry process. For example, as a class, students could brainstorm possible questions and then make predictions. Students are pulling in their prior knowledge of the topic and are

Sample Scenario:

Over the past five years, the world has experienced many weather-related turbulences that have impacted human life. If you turn on any news channel or read any newspaper headline, there are discussions about the threat of global warming. There is significant controversy over the issue of human consumption and global warming, both among scientists and politicians.

Questions such as the following are continually debated:

- Is this because of politics and policy or is global warming really occurring and is human consumption a portion of its cause?
- Is there a relationship among CO_2 emissions and the warming of the earth?

The right questions need to be asked in order to find the right answers. It is your job to discover the truth. Therefore, consider the following:

- Is human consumption of resources causing global warming?
- Is there a relationship or an explanation between global warming and CO_2 emissions?
- Is the tremendous growth and use of resources in developing nations like China having an impact on our climate?
- Are gas guzzling SUVs playing a role?

Findings

In order for your responses to the above questions to be meaningful, they must be well supported. Consider tracking the following data:

- temperature,
- weather patterns and disturbances,
- topography,
- population, and
- automobile statistics over a 10-year time period.

Remember, there may not be definitive answers to the questions that you ask.

Main, open-ended question (the "Hook"):

How much have temperatures increased over the past 10 years around the globe? How fast are temperatures increasing?

Possible sub-questions:
1. What weather disturbances have occurred over the past 10 years around the globe? What has been their frequency? What has been their intensity?

Figure 6.2. Sample Scenario and the "Hook"

2. Based on the data collected, can you predict what will happen in the next 10 years to the global climate?
3. Can you identify any human behavior changes that need to occur as they relate to the global climate?
4. Based on your findings, what will happen to the topography and population in the next 10, 20, and 30 years?

engaged. Another option is to write all student questions on the board. This way there is a record and similarities and differences can be identified for further investigation.

In the question section, you want to make sure that questions posed and predictions made by the students relate to the overall goal of the activity. Keep students focused. The importance of this section is to grab the students' attention and have them identify questions that help them answer your topical question.

It is helpful both to you and the students if you enter the Web inquiry activity with possible questions beyond the topical, main question to help guide your students down the path of inquiry. Inquiry is learned and your role in the process is to ensure that your students begin thinking about the topic and try out new ideas. In a nutshell, you are teaching your students to think.

Guiding Students through the Inquiry Process

Once the topical question has been given, students have asked deeper questions, and predictions have been made, it is now time to provide students with specific steps and strategies to accomplish the task to order to solve the problem. To do this, you need answers for the questions shown below:

- What do you want students to understand?
- How will students best understand the topic?
- What types of data are required?
- How will students demonstrate to others the new knowledge they gained from the activity?

At this stage of the Web inquiry process, your role is to continue to provide guidance by designing an activity that focuses on inquiry, good resources, and presentation of new knowledge. From the students' perspective, once they have asked questions about the topic and discerned possible solutions, the next step is to determine what they need to do to find the best possible answers.

As students begin asking questions they should also begin finding answers, which in turn, leads to new questions. This is the inquiry cycle in action.

For example, data students found indicate that temperatures have been steadily rising over the past 10 years in the Arctic by 2 degrees Celsius.

As a result, follow-up new questions become:

1. Will temperatures in other parts of the world follow this trend?
2. What possible temperature changes do you think will be represented in different parts of the world?
3. Have consumers influenced this trend in rising temperatures?

Figure 6.3.   Other Questions

Exploration of Data

Students use information obtained from the Internet to investigate the topical question and sub-questions. You are preparing students to find reliable and relevant information and ensuring that the information they find is helping them answer the questions. It is important to let students find the resources, but be available with additional resources that they can use if they run into problems.

During this stage, the student investigates and explores online information in an attempt to answer the intended questions. The teacher assists to ensure that the information obtained and reported is accurate and credible.

Analyzing Data

In this section, students manipulate the found data in order to create new knowledge. For example, students collect census data to determine changes in the population over the past ten years. Students can then put these data into a spreadsheet to manipulate the data and draw meaningful conclusions from this new information created.

Needed tools should be made available for students to use as appropriate. For example, if students are looking at textual data, they may need to organize and store information in a database in order to conduct queries to answer important questions.

It is also helpful to provide examples to students on how to manipulate specific types of data in order to answer their identified questions. This helps them to understand the process and why this process of data manipulation is important in solving the intended problem.

Steps to find the information needed:

1. What types of data will I need to find the answers to my questions?
2. What terms do I need to define?
3. What resources are available to me?
4. What types of tools will be needed to manipulate the data?
5. How will I present my manipulated data in order to share it with others?

Types of Data

- National world temperature data
- Influence of temperatures on global weather patterns
- Consumer spending and world temperatures

Defining Important Terms

- Global warming
- Statistical analysis
- Graphing

Resources

- Regional Climate Centers
  http://met-www.cit.cornell.edu/other_rcc.html

- National Oceanographic Data Center
  http://www.nodc.noaa.gov/

- NSF Geosciences Integrated Earth Information Server (IEIS)
  http://atm.geo.nsf.gov/

Tools for Data Manipulation

- Spreadsheet
- Math
- Graphs
- Databases

Figure 6.4. **Providing Guidance through the Inquiry Process**

Presentation of Findings

In the *Findings* section, students communicate with classmates and ultimately the community at large regarding their new findings. This provides relevancy to the activity. Up to this point, students have worked through a structured

Data are placed in a spreadsheet to manipulate. The development of graphs, trend lines, and equations aids in this exploration.

URLs provided:

- Weather database
- Consumer database
- Global warming studies

Web sites provide raw numerical data as well as graphs representing temperature changes over time. Students need to transfer data found into their spreadsheet in order to analyze them further and create their own graphs. Students also need to eliminate any data that are not necessary.

Figure 6.5.   Data Analysis

research process of questioning and then gathering, reflecting, manipulating, and analyzing data.

Now they have the opportunity to share their findings with others. During this section, have your students present, discuss, and defend their results with their classmates and you, the teacher.

It is possible during this section that more questions will be identified, which will open opportunities for further inquiry. Throughout this process, you are teaching your students to solve problems using resources found on the Internet by using a guiding topical question and providing opportunities for students to discover, reflect, investigate, and discuss.

Web Inquiry Templates

A Web inquiry template creates a Teacher Page that outlines the important topical questions and identifies the procedures and the specific strategies students will use during the Web inquiry activity. The Teacher Template is shown below in Figure 6.6.

A Student Page can also be created that identifies the *Hook* and provides the necessary topical questions, possible resources, and guidance for the inquiry process. The Student Template contains only the *Hook*.

CHAPTER SUMMARY

Web inquiry-oriented activities can be used in any subject area and grade level. As discussed above, the idea is for students to use data from the Internet to help answer questions.

The Hook

Identify a topic that allows your students to investigate and explore using Internet resources. The topic must interest them so they ask questions, identify procedures, and conduct a thorough investigation of the problem. Note: This is the only section that students will see.

Identify Questions

Students are responsible for asking further and deeper questions in order to better research their topic, but as the teacher, you must also be prepared with this section.

In this section, list specific focus areas and possible questions. When students run into problems, use these questions to probe and direct them. It is important that students are focused and on task.

Possible Questions

- ...
- ...
- ...
- ...
- ...

Also include sub-questions that you want to ensure are asked. List them here.

- ...
- ...
- ...
- ...

As the teacher, your role is to be the "guide on the side." Your responsibility is to help students through this process; they should be taking the lead.

Identify Good Procedures

Again, this is what your students should be focusing on, but be prepared to offer assistance if needed. The goal is for students to have good inquiry. Here they identify terms, resources, and tools. You can have a list to help guide your students through this process if you think it will help keep them organized.

Data Investigation

Students explore raw unfiltered data. This means that they need to decide what is relevant and what is not. They need to determine how they will transfer the

Figure 6.6. Teacher Template

data found into a tool that will help them pull it apart and identify key elements. Some guidance from you may be needed at this stage.

Have a list of Web sites and tools for students to use. Keep students focused on the questions to help determine what data are needed.

Analysis

Raw data need to be manipulated before they can be used to answer identified questions. You may need to provide examples on how students can manipulate their found data to help answer their specific questions.

Data can be manipulated by using Excel or mind mapping tools.

Findings

Consider how you want your students to present their findings to others. Results may not be possible, but findings should be well supported from information gathered.

In this section, students may have no clear cut answers but they should have identified further investigation and questions. They should list them in their presentation. This begins the inquiry cycle all over again.

Figure 6.6.   (*continued*)

Title

Author(s) Names

Author(s) Contact Information

Hook

- Grab your students' interest.
- Create a hook that students are interested in and want to investigate further.
- Encourage students to ask deeper questions to help guide their inquiry.

Figure 6.7.   Student Template

Traditional lessons have typically involved already found and put together filtered sources from textbooks, videos, or lectures. When we incorporate the Internet and bring inquiry into the classroom, we provide students the opportunity to tie real-world elements into the curriculum and content.

Web inquiry activities engage and interest students and, at the same time, provide a foundation to help build connections and meaning. Web inquiry allows students to ask good questions, make predictions, determine relevancy, and present this new information to others.

CHAPTER REFLECTION

1. How is a Web inquiry activity different from a WebQuest?
2. Why should students only see the *Hook* in a Web inquiry activity?
3. What is significant about a Web inquiry activity for the student?
4. What is the role of the teacher in a Web inquiry activity?
5. Why is manipulating raw and unfiltered data important for students?

SKILL-BUILDING ACTIVITY

This chapter explored how to create a Web inquiry activity. The focus was on engaging students into a topical question so they are motivated to conduct research and discover new information. Throughout this process, students identify deeper questions and then find raw data on the Internet to help answer those questions. They choose appropriate data, manipulate the data, create possible solutions, and present their findings to others. Your goal is to create a Web inquiry activity that aligns with your learning standards and is developed around an interesting and doable topical question. You want to identify possible procedures, resources, and tools that your students need to complete this inquiry activity. Remember that you only provide the *Hook* to your students while being open to assisting and supporting them in difficult areas.

Chapter Seven

Creating a Telecollaborative Activity

A telecollaborative activity provides opportunities for students to work and create information with other students or experts in different geographical locations using online communication tools such as LISTSERVs, message boards, real-time chat, and Web-based conferencing. Locations can be as close as down the hall or as far away as around the world.

The benefits of telecollaborative activities are the ability to connect through the Internet with other students, teachers, researchers, scientists, politicians, and business leaders around the world. This connection is made possible through the Web.

In this chapter, we identify and explore telecollaborative activities that can be implemented in your classroom. We start with a "big idea" question and then move on to create activities that require participation and engagement from outside participants. You can create your own telecollaborative activity or you can participate in an activity that has already been created by someone else. Either way, telecollaboration is a terrific learning experience for you and your students.

OVERVIEW

Telecollaboration provides opportunities for students to practice inquiry learning through the process of questioning, reflecting, and manipulating information using the Internet by collaborating and communicating with others. Students work as a collaborative group to explore and collect information. They then share this new information with other classrooms and experts all around the world using telecommunication.

Telecollaborative activities are curriculum based, teacher designed, and co-ordinated. Most have Web sites to share information collected and information about the activity itself. A telecollaborative activity is usually integrated directly into the curriculum and is not an extra activity.

As with any inquiry-oriented activity, your goal as the teacher is to engage your students with a "big idea" question and then let them discover workable answers. The difference between a telecollaborative activity and other inquiry-oriented activities explored throughout this book thus far is the opportunity for students to now work with other students and/or experts in the field around the globe on authentic and meaningful problems.

In a telecollaborative activity, your students collect raw data and then share their information. Once the information is shared, other students and/or experts have the ability to further explore the collection of data to solve problems.

For example, assume you are planning a unit on the Revolutionary War in your social studies class. A typical lesson on this unit may have students read a chapter on the Revolutionary War and then go to the library to find further information on the war so they can write a report for the class.

An enhancement to this activity could include a telecollaborative element by having your students work with another class in a different part of the world.

You would begin by:

- Collecting primary-source documents on the Revolutionary War from the American Memory Project at http://memory.loc.gov;
- Outlining a debate topic; and
- Contacting teachers on ePals at http://www.epals.com to see who would be interested in working with you on a debate related to the Revolutionary War with both of your classes.

A teacher from England responds to your inquiry, agreeing to a classroom debate on a specific "big idea" question such as: *Can a compromise be reached before the war begins?* (between the two sides in the Revolutionary War). Imagine the experiences your students will receive debating, via the Internet, during a peace conference with a class from England on Revolutionary War issues and topics.

The varying perspectives and resources submitted from both classes as well as the awe of the long-distance link are noteworthy. Information gleaned from the classroom debate can be collected on a shared Web site where both classes can add to the information and make changes. In addition, lessons learned can be documented as well as the potential for ongoing dialog with this international classroom.

The above is a good illustrative example of a telecollaborative activity where teachers and students from different geographic locations and cultures have the opportunity to work together on a problem or shared experience.

As introduced above, you have two choices. Your class can either join a telecollaborative activity or you as the teacher can create a telecollaborative activity and invite other classes to participate. Both approaches are discussed in this chapter.

USING THE INTERNET IN A TELECOLLABORATIVE ACTIVITY

When implementing telecollaboration into your classroom, the Internet is the central tool. The Internet helps classes and experts share information and ideas through collaboration and communication, using tools such as e-mail, teleconferencing, and chat.

You want to explore ways information can be shared and then assess what types of technology tools you currently have available for use as well as what tools you think might be needed when implementing this activity in your classroom.

TYPES OF TOOLS

When you look for possible telecollaborative activities to join or when you create a telecollaborative activity of your own, you want to investigate ways information can be exchanged using the Internet. Information can be transferred via the Internet through interpersonal communication (e-mail), appearances (Web-based conferencing), and mentoring (real-time chat). Figure 7.1 provides a graphic of this connection.

Interpersonal activities allow students to actively communicate with other participants using either e-mail on an asynchronous basis (not at the same time) or chat, which is used synchronously (at the same time). By using e-mail or chat, you have many possibilities for interaction through specific settings or environments.

A global classroom is a type of collaborative environment that utilizes a Web site and has all the necessary tools for communication and collaboration to take place. Within this environment, classes can post documents, data, and e-mail or chat with different users. An example of a global classroom is the United Nations Global Classroom found at http://www.unausa.org/global-classrooms-model-un.

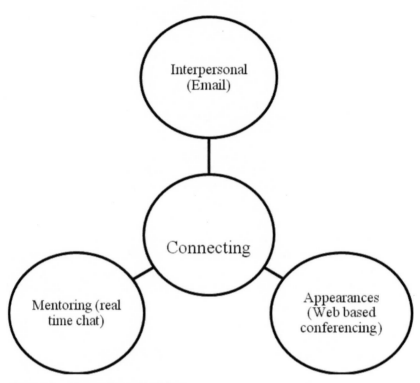

Figure 7.1.   Connecting with Others

Another type of environment is an electronic appearance. These are typically online workshops led and conducted by experts in the field. These appearances are guided by authors or scientists and allow students to ask questions in order to examine parts of a text or discuss and analyze new and interesting concepts, such as the latest science invention.

Electronic mentoring is another opportunity for students to ask questions of subject matter experts from both industry and business. Students have an opportunity to ask questions so that they can answer their own questions to help solve a problem. These experts help with the telecollaborative activity directly.

Question-and-answer services, such as Ask an Expert at http://www.ask .com/ or the Mad Sci Network at http://www.madsci.org/, provide opportunities for students to ask specific and well thought out questions about problems that they have researched and need help in finding answers.

In each of these collaborative interactions, communication around specific topics as well as working with others, including experts in the field and at a distance, is the central focus. In order to make a telecollaborative activity beneficial for your class you must prepare for these interactions and ensure your students have opportunities for communication and problem solving.

TYPES OF ACTIVITIES

Once you have determined the types and methods of communication, the next step is to identify some possible activities for students to participate in. It is important that the activity tie into a specific learning goal. Usually, any learning goal that allows students to practice inquiry skills can be incorporated into this activity.

There are various types of inquiry-oriented activities that can be integrated into a telecollaborative activity. For example, information collection and analysis allows students to collect, compare, contrast, and synthesize complex information that they have collected and evaluated. This information can be posted for other classrooms around the world to access and evaluate. Generally, information collection and analysis involves an online database that can be accessed by all and queried.

Problem-solving activities can also be used. They provide students with a complex problem that encourages them to critically analyze and synthesize information. This information can be primary or secondary and they must use this information to present meaningful solutions.

Types of problem-solving activities include social action projects, peer feedback activities, and information exchanges. In each type, students examine a problem, such as high gas prices, and then use data to determine the best solution for the stakeholders, in this case both the local and global economy.

Whether collecting and analyzing information or problem solving, as the teacher your role is to encourage and guide your students. You also provide varied and engaging opportunities for them to research appropriate resources and compile worthwhile information so others can work with the information and help determine possible solutions.

In order for your telecollaborative activity to be successful, there are a few items to consider. Remember to:

1. Identify appropriate learning goals and objectives that tie into your standards of learning (SOLs);
2. Find a partner class or an expert in the field; and
3. Develop specific and planned procedures, e.g.,
   - Identify how the expert and/or classes will work together;
   - Identify and collect necessary content and resources;
   - Identify specific benchmark dates for data collection, sharing, and presentation; and

- Provide opportunities for reflection and feedback for you and your students throughout the process.

In a telecollaborative activity, students have opportunities to work on similar activities in different locations, cultures, and time zones. This is a major strength of this activity, but it also takes planning and specific benchmarks to accomplish your goals.

To help prepare, ensure that your specific benchmark dates as well as your reflection and feedback opportunities are varied and manageable. This assists students and/or experts at each location in collecting and sharing information online so that the information is available for all participants to analyze and evaluate.

For example, assume you are a science teacher and your goal is to have students think locally as well as globally about the environment and earth systems. In deciding on a telecollaborative activity, you begin by conducting an Internet search and find a Web resource at the Global Learning and Observations to Benefit the Environment (GLOBE) Web site at http://www.globe.gov.

After reviewing the GLOBE Web site, you become aware that teachers and students from around the world are already conducting primary research and collaborating with scientists from both the National Aeronautics and Space Administration (NASA) and the National Science Association (NSA). You decide to have your class participate.

As part of the project, it is your responsibility to work with your students to collect quality data in your local area on a specific plant and animal group that is outlined on the GLOBE Web site. Once your class collects the appropriate data, they import the information into the GLOBE database. There are specific benchmarks that must be met so the data can be used by classrooms around the world as well as by NASA and NSA scientists to create a satellite map of specific animal and plant populations around the world.

This example demonstrates the collaborative nature of the telecollaborative activity from the standpoint that your students' efforts impact the work of real-world scientists and researchers. Quality data are collected and inputted so that they are available for meaningful interpretation and analysis.

As this example highlights, other classrooms and scientists are counting on your students to help build knowledge and fill the database with quality data in a timely manner so real-world predictions and discoveries can be made. This is a true real-world partnership.

THINKING TELECOLLABORATIVELY

The Internet is a powerful tool for schools and classrooms. It provides global resources that are timely and abundant. Most importantly, it provides access to classrooms and experts around the world on topics that are real and relevant to students and the overall curriculum. A telecollaborative activity combines the benefit of Internet resources with the collaboration and sharing of information.

In order to participate, your classroom needs access to an Internet connection, a meaningful and appropriate project that meets your curriculum needs, and necessary tools to analyze, communicate, synthesize, and share information, such as a spreadsheet, word processing, e-mail, and presentation tools.

Start by providing your students with a relevant problem that is real world and meaningful, and that can be investigated. Next, start exploring other classrooms and experts that would like to participate.

As mentioned above, when working with others outside of the classroom, time is an important consideration. Time must be provided for students to collect data and to provide thoughtful reflection about the data that will ultimately be shared with participating classes. Also, school schedules or schedules of experts must be considered and accounted for when designing or planning to participate in a telecollaborative activity.

When you integrate a telecollaborative activity into your classroom, you are no longer using the Internet solely as a library research tool. Now you are moving your students toward using the Internet as a critical-thinking and communication tool.

For example, in the telecollaborative activity, Underground Railroad found at http://exchange.co-nect.net/Teleprojects/project/?pid=, the year is 1850. Students work in collaborative teams and share information with other classes in different locations through a discussion forum.

The length of time for this telecollaborative activity is fifteen days and the journey requires students to explore, collect, and then share experiences on a group discussion board with classes also taking this journey in different locations around the world.

Planning is important so that students can explore the content provided in this activity and then share their data and experiences with other participating classrooms. The research and time spent interacting with other classes to discuss issues, process, and identify problems and concerns all need to be considered in terms of deciding time allotments and constraints.

HOW TO PLAN FOR A TELECOLLABORATIVE ACTIVITY

Planning involves identifying specific learning objectives and goals. It also includes setting explicit benchmarks for students to collect, analyze, and then share their data with others. In addition, planning time is also spent finding a topic and identifying a specific product that engages your students and increases their understanding of your content area.

When starting the planning process, first begin by looking at your curriculum. Start by outlining course topics and themes that you will be covering throughout the school year.

As you identify main topics and key themes, ideas for a telecollaborative activity that you can participate in or create for your students should become apparent. Planning always begins by looking at your topics and themes. Next, identify specific standards of learning.

Figure 7.3 highlights the learning topics and themes that you identified in Figure 7.2 and incorporates appropriate learning standards. When searching for and/or creating a telecollaborative activity, these areas should always be recognized.

Course topics to be covered during the academic year:

1.

2.

3.

4.

5.

6.

7.

8.

9.

10.

From this list, identify three possible themes:

1.

2.

3.

Figure 7.2.   Identify Topics and Themes

Standards of Learning:

Topic(s):

Theme(s):

Learning Standards:

Figure 7.3. Identify Learning Standards

Identify Computer Hardware and Software Needed

When joining a telecollaborative activity developed by another teacher, identify what types of computer hardware and software are necessary to participate and make sure your school has the necessary tools. Figure 7.4 provides a checklist of some possible tools that you may need access to. Double check this worksheet when you find a telecollaborative activity to participate in to ensure that you have the necessary tools.

TYPES OF TELECOLLABORATIVE ACTIVITIES

There are many different types of telecollaborative activities with varying ways to share information with others. As such, you should be able to find activities that meet your learning and curriculum needs. Each of the possibilities outlined in Figure 7.5 below can be combined or completed as stand-alone individual activities.

The following are two main types of telecollaborative activities—learning opportunities and data collection—that will allow your students to learn content as well as help you identify specific activities to implement that will work well with your class.

In each learning opportunity presented in a telecollaborative activity, students are able to practice Internet research as well as evaluate information obtained online. Students also have the opportunity to explore relevant topics and can help find answers to specific questions.

An important element of a telecollaborative activity is that students explore and review varying answers and perspectives to the same question and practice information-seeking and information-evaluating skills. Information seeking is when students investigate and explore topics using research methods. Information evaluating is when students evaluate found information to make sure it is reliable and valid.

Computer Hardware

1. Operating System

   Windows, Mac, Linux, Other _____

2. RAM _____ (MB/GB)

3. Hard Drive _____ (MB/GB)

4. Processor (Ghz) _____

5. Internet Connection (circle the correct connection)

   Dial Up/Modem, Network, Other _____

6. Digital Camera _____

7. Scanner _____

8. Microphone _____

9. Sound Card _____

10. Digital Video Camera/Web Cam _____

11. Audio Visual Capabilities (Card) _____

Computer Software

1. Word Processing _____

2. Spreadsheet _____

3. Database _____

4. Image Editing _____

5. Presentation _____

6. Video Editing Software _____

7. Web Page Editor _____

8. Draw/Paint _____

Other

1.

2.

3.

Figure 7.4.   **Computer Hardware and Software Checklist**

Learning Opportunities

- Information Exchange

    - Provides opportunities for your class to share specific and personal information of the class or location via e-mail with other classes.

    For example, your class may be studying a language or a culture and could e-mail a student or class from that particular country or culture.

- Data Collection

    - Students collect, analyze, and compare different types of information.

    - Examples include opportunities for students to complete a questionnaire or to track specific events by collecting primary data.

    - For example, students collect data on Monarch butterflies to identify specific migration paths.

    - Or, students collect local weather data to compile a database on national weather patterns.

Figure 7.5.   Learning Opportunities

When identifying activities that are beneficial to student learning, it is important to choose appropriate learning opportunities centered on student activities. See Figure 7.6 for sample telecollaborative activities.

There are many ways that students can present information to others. It can be done through:

- written format, such as through letters and stories;
- data analysis and organization, using spreadsheets, graphs, and charts;
- visually, through the use of images and drawings;
- auditory, with narration and music; or
- through multimedia, combining each of these elements plus adding animation.

Each of these communication types allows your students to convey meaning to the information collected and analyzed.

In the planning process, identify ways students can communicate and exchange information and files. Students can create a Web site, attach files to e-mail, use file transfer protocol to transfer files from one server to another,

- Newly developed products by those participating in the telecollaborative activity give students an opportunity to create something and then share it with others.

  - For example, students collaborate with other classes around the world to write a specific chapter in a novel about a historical event.

- Primary research opportunities provide students with opportunities to work on complex problems that may not have specific answers. Students are responsible for developing and comprehending possible hypotheses, identifying necessary resources, collecting data, and then analyzing and manipulating the data by synthesizing the information and then reporting their findings to the collective telecollaborative group.

  - For example, students participate and compete in a ThinkQuest project where students in different global classrooms create an activity to be used in lessons.

- Real time conferencing with experts and other students in different parts of the world is a way for classrooms to communicate.

  - Conferencing can be through chat or video.

  - Students log on to talk with specific classrooms and experts to share and synthesize data, as well as present new and relevant information.

Figure 7.6.   Different Types of Activities

input data into an online database, or use conferencing tools that are cross platform in order to communicate and share files with a wider audience.

Whether you participate in an existing telecollaborative activity or you create an activity yourself, the following guidelines are recommended:

- The activity meets your identified curriculum goals and objectives.
- Students have opportunities to solve real-world problems that are meaningful to them.
- The topic and themes are integrated seamlessly throughout the activity in order for students to build knowledge and skills based on your identified standards of learning.
- The activity engages and motivates students through the discovery of information and connecting information to prior knowledge.
- Students have opportunities to communicate with others outside of the classroom, such as other students or experts in the field, to test their hypotheses.

- Students employ critical-thinking skills, such as comparing and contrasting, analyzing data, researching with primary data, conducting discussions and reflecting on these discussions, and identifying fact from opinion.
- Students have opportunities to be self-directed in their own learning and as a result begin to develop skills in problem solving.

In short, the telecollaborative activity facilitates active student participation from all students, regardless of location. In addition, it is meaningful and allows for hands-on participation and engagement from all students.

Existing Telecollaborative Activities

Up to this point in the chapter, we have explored different telecollaborative activities and multiple ways to communicate and share information. This section focuses on participation in an existing telecollaborative activity.

Joining an existing activity before creating your own activity provides you with the benefit of learning best practices and what it takes to be successful when working with the Internet as a tool for data collection, dissemination, and collaboration with others at different locations around the world.

When researching telecollaborative activities to use in your classroom, start by looking at specific directories and e-mail list projects to find a good activity that is appropriate for your students and content area. In your search, you will find both free and pay-for-service activities. Some examples include:

- iEARN: A non-profit global network that allows teachers and students to collaborate on real-world issues and concerns using the Internet (available at http://www.iearn.org/).
- Global SchoolNet: Links classrooms around the world with activities and projects that make a difference on a global scale (available at http://www.globalschoolnet.org/index.cfm).
- TEAMS Education Resources: A Resource Page provided by the Los Angeles County Office of Education (available at http://teams.lacoe.edu/documentation/projects/projects.html).
- ePals: An e-mail service for teachers to identify possible telecollaborative activities with classrooms around the world (available at http://www.epals.com/).
- International Telementoring Program: Provides mentoring opportunities for classrooms around the world from leaders in business and industry (available at http://www.telementor.org/).

When you first begin a telecollaborative activity, it is best to start small. For example, consider exploring an activity that involves using e-mail to exchange a message or to share information about your community or class. The Global Grocery Project at http://landmark-project.com/ggl/index.html lets students collect data and add their own data to an online database that records local grocery prices.

These types of introductory activities allow you and your students to experience a telecollaborative activity without an extensive time or resource commitment. Once you and your students become comfortable collecting and sharing information, you can grow to larger and more involved activities.

When first starting out, it can also be helpful to find another teacher at your school who wants to participate. Another option is to include your technology-resource teacher. It is important to have assistance, especially with larger and more involved projects, and to know what resources you need and what you have available for use. If you are missing something, can you survive? And if not, you need to determine how you will obtain the necessary resources to be successful.

It is important to identify your technology skill level and determine what assistance you need to complete the activity. Do not be afraid to ask for help. Your technology-resource teacher is an excellent resource. Remember also that other classrooms are counting on the data that your students collect and share, so make sure that you are prepared and have the necessary support to be successful.

Designing a Telecollaborative Activity

As you design your own telecollaborative activity, view some existing projects to give you ideas. When planning and developing your activity, be mindful that you are writing for fellow teachers, not your students. Fellow teachers review the activity guidelines and expectations to determine if they want their class to participate.

During this initial design phase, identify possible participants, such as earth science classes or English literature classes. You do not necessarily have to work with classes in your same subject area and can branch out to cross-curricular participation to incorporate more dynamic data.

In designing your own telecollaborative activity, below are some guiding points. Identify these points in your lesson write-up so other teachers can determine if the activity meets their specific learning goals and needs.

Identify your learning goals and objectives. What activities will be online to learn this new information? Is this an appropriate way for students to achieve these goals? Identify your appropriate standards of learning (SOLs). Do they match what you intend for students to learn?

Ensure that the activity is easy to implement and continue throughout its duration. Telecollaborative activities involve more than your class. They also involve telecommunications and media tools for both teaching and learning. Is your idea appropriate for these tools and this type of learning?

Actively involve students throughout the activity with ample opportunity for hands-on experience. Have you provided quality activities that serve each learning objective? Are the activities allowing students to think critically about the content?

Collaborate with other classes, schools, or experts in the field of study. Build in opportunities for continued communication with all participants. Clearly and specifically identify how each participant will communicate and exchange information, such as via e-mail, a discussion forum, a LISTSERV, or Web-based chat.

Identify specific hardware or software requirements. Another important introductory element is a clear and doable timeline that includes specific benchmarks for each participant for the duration of the project.

Include continuous and appropriate student assessment and evaluation throughout the activity. Provide clear and doable benchmarks for all participants to follow. Communicate in a timely manner to all participants regarding the closing date of the project and the results of the data obtained once compiled and evaluated.

Once these guidelines are completed, you can prepare your project goals, topic, theme, and requirements. Make sure that the information is clear for all participants to follow.

Next, determine how you will compile and distribute the results to the participants once the activity has concluded. And finally, identify both formal and informal methods of evaluation of student work.

Ensure that you have enough participants for your activity to gather suitable data. Some will drop out or not submit all data sets, so make sure your activity is long enough and has enough participants to pull good information from your data. Conversely, if your activity has too many participants, this can also be a problem. Strive for a balance.

As you work with other participants, make sure to maintain continued and open contact. Meet all set deadlines and remind participants of deadlines and benchmarks. Motivate your students as well as the other participants by letting them know that this is an important activity and the work that they are doing is meaningful and worth the effort.

Be flexible. We all have technology issues and may not be aware of these issues when we begin the activity. Ensure that you have the technical support needed to answer questions and help with alternative solutions if need be.

A sample telecollaborative activity is outlined in Figure 7.7.

Activity Title: Revolutionary War Peace Conference

Project Description:

- Students participating in the Revolutionary War Peace Conference are delegates who will represent opposite points of view on events leading up to the Revolutionary War.

- Students compare and contrast views on the American Revolution from the viewpoint of the monarchy in England as well as the Virginia settlers in the new world.

- Several important issues should be explored by each point of view (above), including:
  - fiscal matters,
  - the English monarchy,
  - concerns for liberty,
  - the Constitution of 1787, and
  - anti-federalism.

- As delegates, students are assigned by the leaders during this time period to help settle their differences. Can it be done?

- Each presentation must highlight the viewpoints of the respective group using video conferencing and e-pals.

- Delegates from both points of view will present their arguments, debate, and then decide whether a compromise can be reached.

- Delegates will vote to determine the appropriate wording for the treaty. Hopefully, the Peace Conference is successful!

Instructional Goal(s):

- The overarching goal is for students to learn more about their national heritage and other cultures to become more knowledgeable global citizens.

- During this process of discovery and debate, students begin to understand chronological thinking, connection between causes and effects, and the connection between continuity and change.

- Students also begin the exploration of personal responsibility and that ideas, opinions, and experiences have real consequences.

- Through this process of discovery, students understand that events are shaped both by ideas and the actions of the individual.

Figure 7.7.   Sample Telecollaborative Activity

Grade Level: Elementary and Middle School

Contact information of organizer (Name, e-mail, address, phone number, etc.):

Subject Areas: History, Social Science, Geography, Civics, Economics

Learning Standards:

History and Social Science

- Analyze the forces of conflict and cooperation.

- Develop skills in discussion, debate, and persuasive writing with respect to enduring issues and determine how divergent viewpoints have been addressed and reconciled.

- Compare and contrast fundamental political principles including:
  - constitutionalism and limited government,
  - rule of law,
  - democracy and republicanism,
  - sovereignty,
  - consent of the governed,
  - separation of powers,
  - checks and balances, and
  - federalism.

- Compare and contrast fundamental liberties, rights, and values including:
  - religion,
  - speech,
  - press,
  - assembly and petition,
  - due process,
  - equality under the law,
  - individual worth and dignity,
  - majority rule, and
  - minority rights.

- Demonstrate skills in historical research and geographical analysis by identifying, analyzing, and interpreting primary and secondary sources and artifacts as well as validating sources as to their authenticity, authority, credibility, and possible bias.

Language Arts

- Identify main ideas and concepts presented in resources.

- Draw inferences, conclusions, or generalizations about text and support them with textual evidence and prior knowledge.

- Distinguish facts, supported inferences, and opinions in text.

- Use organizational features of printed text (e.g., citations, end notes, and bibliographic references) to locate relevant information.

Number of Participants Needed for This Activity: Two classrooms

Estimated Time: Two weeks, including time to prepare and present.

Prior Learning:

Prior to this lesson, students need to understand the events leading up to the American Revolution and identify recurring themes and/or inconsistencies found in resources.

Directions for Joining the Activity:

This telecollaborative activity will bring together American students with students in England. ePals will be used to gather and share information and a video teleconference will be implemented at the end for a Peace Conference Debate.

Hardware and Software Requirements:

Specific software and hardware that will be used for the duration of this activity:

- Telecommunications:
  Required: ePals, Web-based conferencing
  Optional: video conferencing

- Hardware:
  Required: PC, Mac, Linux
  Optional:

- Software:
  Required: e-mail, word processor, concept map
  Optional: video software

- Other:
  Required:
  Optional:

Possible Resources:

Folk Music of England http://www.contemplator.com/war.html

Music of the American Revolution http://members.aol.com/bobbyj164/mrev .htm

Figure 7.7. (*continued*)

Spy Letters http://www.si.umich.edu/spies/

George Washington Papers http://lcweb2.loc.gov/ammem/gwhtml/gwhome
.html, http://gwpapers.virginia.edu/

Queen Charlotte Letters http://people.virginia.edu/~jlc5f/charlotte/charlett5
.html

Revolutionary War Timeline http://www.nps.gov/archive/cowp/Timeline.htm

Map Collection http://memory.loc.gov/ammem/gmdhtml/armhtml/

Continental Congress http://memory.loc.gov/ammem/collections/continental/

PBS American Revolution http://www.pbs.org/ktca/liberty/

Process:

- Task: Students identify major events, themes, and inconsistencies found in resources about the American Revolutionary War.
- Any resource on the Revolutionary War can be used, including textbooks.
- Students organize information gathered in order to compare and contrast information and set up an argument to prevent the Revolutionary War.
- On the final day of this activity, students participate in a debate with the opposing side to convince the leaders not to go into war.

Lesson Preparation

- Search for reliable information on the Revolutionary War
- Identify recurring themes and possible inconsistencies
- Small groups will identify specific causes leading to the war
- Small groups will identify possible solutions to these issues
- Approximate time: 1 week

ePals Registration

- Teacher registers project with ePals and locates another teacher or classroom who can participate in this project
- Students are introduced to the other class through e-mail

American Revolution Folders

- Teachers prepare ways for students to organize information during the duration of the project such as using folders, social bookmarking, Web sites, and a database.
- Students collect, analyze, and present information on the events, issues, and causes of the American Revolution.

Day 1
Introduction:

Introduce students to the assignment and procedures/guidelines for this telecollaborative project.

Big Idea Question:

Can you stop the American Revolutionary War?

You will look at what happened. Is there a compromise that could have been reached before the war began? What event or issue could have been prevented from happening?

Meet the Correspondent:

Each class will e-mail the following information about each of the students in the class:

1. Name
2. Age
3. Hometown and Country
4. School
5. Hobbies
6. Fun Facts
7. Other Pertinent Information

Events That Brought about the American Revolution:

- Students will e-mail the other class regarding important events that brought about the American Revolution as presented by their history textbooks.

- Students identify political, religious, and economic ideas and interests that brought about the Revolution, such as the resistance to imperial policy, the Stamp Act, the Townshend Acts, taxes on tea, Coercive Acts, etc.

- Create a concept map to share with the other class to identify key issues and their understanding about each.

Day 2
Drafting and Signing of the Declaration of Independence

- Who were the people and the events associated with this document?
- Why was this document important?
- What did signing this document say to the monarchy in England?

- Share findings through e-mail

Figure 7.7. (*continued*)

- Identify key points made by both classes
- Add artifacts and findings into a database for easy retrieval
- Save resources

Day 3
- Who were the people making decisions and influencing policy during this time period?

- Share findings through e-mail
- Identify key points made by both classes
- Add artifacts and findings into a database for easy retrieval
- Save resources

Day 4
- Identify battles, campaigns, and varying turning points within this time period

- Share findings through e-mail
- Identify key points made by both classes
- Add artifacts and findings into a database for easy retrieval
- Save resources

Day 5
- What are the specific roles of the British, American, and Indian leaders during this time period?

- Share findings through e-mail
- Identify key points made by both classes
- Add artifacts and findings into a database for easy retrieval
- Save resources

Day 6
- What were the economic hardships of the everyday person living during this time period? Include families, financing the war, inflation, hoarding goods for profiteering, etc.

- Share findings through e-mail
- Identify key points made by both classes
- Add artifacts and findings into a database for easy retrieval
- Save resources

Day 7
- Compile data and identify an outline for the debate
- Share findings through e-mail
- Both classes will determine key issues to debate and a time schedule for each side
- Share artifacts and resources with the other class
- Save resources

Days 8 and 9
- Prepare debate around outlined topics and issues
- Students can use any media to help convey message, e.g., images, video, animation, text, etc.

Day 10
- Debate via video conference
- Post lesson wrap-up
- Final e-mail
- After the debate, have students write a final e-mail identifying key take aways and a final thank you for the effort and work on this collaborative project

Evaluation of Student Learning:

The evaluation of this project is based on the final research project and whether students were able to effectively compare and contrast information about the American Revolution.

The following is a rubric that can be used to assess the final research report:

4 (Exceeds Standards)	• Identifies key issues, views, and important events of the American Revolution.
	• Identifies points of view from different sides.
	• Supports views with quality resources.
	• Provides a solid argument for viewpoint, identifying quality resources to include primary source documents and historians.
	• Well prepared for debate.
• 3 (At Standard)	• Supports ideas for varying viewpoints.
	• Able to identify inferences, conclusions, or generalizations about resources and is able to support with good resources and prior knowledge.
	• Able to identify some facts, supported inferences, and opinions in resources.
	• Uses varying methods to organize and display information, concept maps, database, images, word processing, etc.

Figure 7.7. (*continued*)

- Supports argument with well-researched ideas surrounding issues and events.

2 (Approaching Standard)
- Able to identify some main ideas and concepts presented in resources.

- Able to draw some inferences, conclusions, or generalizations about resources as well as some textual evidence and prior knowledge.

- Identifies some facts, inferences, and opinions in resources accurately.

- Organizes information well by using some tools to convey meaning of information gathered.

- Supports argument to some extent.

1 (Does Not Meet Standard)
- Identifies few main ideas, concepts, and issues within quality resources.

- Identifies only a few inferences, conclusions, or generalizations about resources and is not able to support them with textual evidence and prior knowledge.

- Identifies a few to no facts, supported inferences, and opinions in text.

- Does not use very many organization methods and does not locate quality information.

- Does not support argument well.

Evaluating Your Telecollaborative Activity

After developing and creating a telecollaborative activity, it is important to evaluate its effectiveness to ensure that you are meeting your learning goals and emphasizing the collaboration and communication tools available to you. In evaluating your activity, ensure that:

- it aligns with the appropriate learning objectives and goals;
- it is realistic and doable; and
- your activities are clearly outlined and appropriately sequenced.

Table 7.1. Evaluate Your Activity

Evaluate Your Activity:	*Yes/No*
Learning objectives identified	
Learning goal is clear and accurate	
Standards of learning align with activity	
Are the activities realistic and doable?	
Are the activities clearly aligned with the learning objectives?	
Are the activities appropriately sequenced?	
Can this activity be done better without collaborating with others outside of the classroom?	

Activity Title:

Project Description:

Instructional Goal(s):

Contact information of organizer (Name, e-mail, address, phone number, etc.):

Grade Level:

Subject Areas:

Standards of Learning:

Identify expected prior knowledge of learners:

Who should consider participating?

Number of participants accepted for activity:

Directions for joining the activity:

Specific software and hardware that will be used for the duration of activity:
Resources:

Process (specific):

Evaluation of student learning:

Figure 7.8. Telecollaborative Lesson Template

Telecollaborative Activity Template

The following is a telecollaborative activity template that you can use in developing your activities.

CHAPTER SUMMARY

Telecollaborative activities are a great way to utilize the communication and collaboration tools of the Internet. The purpose of a telecollaborative activity is to effectively use the Internet to engage learners by working with other classes or with experts in the field of study using real-world tools. It is a very effective learning tool for engaging students in the inquiry learning process with participants outside of the classroom.

CHAPTER REFLECTION

1. How could you integrate a telecollaborative activity into your curriculum?
2. Identify types of learning opportunities and activities that would be beneficial to your students' learning and your own standards of learning (SOLs) for your topic.
3. What are some of the key components to a successful telecollaborative project?

SKILL-BUILDING ACTIVITIES

1. You have explored telecollaborative activities in this chapter; now it is time to begin researching telecollaborative activities that you can participate in with your students. Remember to start simple and grow in difficulty and involvement. You may want to begin with a project using e-mail correspondence. Review the ePals Web site at http://www.epals .com and see if there is an introductory activity that would be interesting for your class.
2. Now that you have participated in a simple activity, it is time to begin the process of finding and participating in a more involved activity. This could be one or two weeks in duration and involve students collecting and sharing data. Find something that is doable and not too overwhelming. Remember that other classes or experts are depending on you, so make sure that you can meet each benchmark.

3. For this third activity, try creating your own telecollaborative project. Identify your learning standards, topics, and resources. Next, determine what activities will help your students meet each of these standards using telecommunication tools. Document your activity and begin seeking participants. Post on a telecollaborative LISTSERV such as Classroom Projects at http://www.globalschoolnet.org/. Or post your activity on ePals at http://www.epals.com/, KidLink at http://www.kidlink.org/, or the Kid Link Project Center at http://www.kidlink.org/drupal/project/.

Chapter Eight

Creating a Problem-Based Activity

Problem-based learning presents a dynamic method to provide students the opportunity to explore a real-world problem or challenge around a curricular topic. As students investigate this "messy" problem, they can work in small collaborative groups with problem strands that reach across the curriculum.

When designing a problem-based lesson activity, it is best practice to incorporate challenges around the lesson objectives. By doing so, students develop critical-thinking skills. Emphasis is placed on situated learning, e.g., learning takes place in a specific learning situation and the time spent learning is dependent on the environment itself.

OVERVIEW

Problem-based activities include a variety of different approaches. To provide an initial example, a good illustration to lay the foundation would be students creating a historical newspaper. In this activity, students practice writing and research skills, as well as develop presentation skills. In addition, in many problem-based activities, the teacher has the opportunity to learn along with the students.

In this activity, students are divided into small groups of approximately three to four students each. Within each group, students select a historical date or an event, and a historical city to report on.

Depending on your groups and curricular topics being studied, the historical event or time period can incorporate other countries. A telecollaborative activity (see chapter 7) could also be included in the lesson with students from different countries working together to write the newspaper. Students from each country could then compare and contrast the differing views and events.

The task is to design and develop a newspaper that could have been published in a particular city after a specific date or event. In keeping authentic to the time period, students produce a newspaper in historical style and form.

The next major task is for the group to select a name for their newspaper. Each group member is responsible for maintaining the authenticity of the design to include text and images.

Each group member then selects a particular content area or section of the newspaper to write. This can include the main story, world news, local or regional news, music, sports, science, advertisements, etc. In order to write and present the newspaper section, students conduct research by reviewing primary-source documents and then edit their work in preparation for peer review.

During the formative evaluation of their peers, feedback is provided on the content and writing of each group member's work. Once completed, copies are made to distribute to the teacher, library, and other groups.

At the conclusion of the project, each group presents a poster session that represents their contributions to the project. Each team can bring in historical artifacts or develop a replica of an artifact. Groups interact with the poster presentation and the class learns more about a given time period or event.

An evaluation rubric that identifies the key areas of assessment, historical research, writing, collaborative work, design and production, and the whole-class presentation can be created and utilized. The activity is open-ended, e.g., students can select any noteworthy event and corresponding city location that interests them, but planning is necessary to ensure students receive clear guidelines of each intended expectation.

Helpful guidelines in the planning process include:

- Establishing a time frame (to include time spent during class and length of time to complete);
- Determining the group selection process;
- Preparing an assessment rubric;
- Selecting events and time period (Can there be more than one group working on the same event or time period?);
- Determining topic selection (Can students choose their own topic within a time period or section in the newspaper?);
- Evaluating research (What types of research should students use to find information about their topic and time period?);
- Setting up a presentation (What should students cover?); and
- Length of newspaper or article

Throughout this problem-based activity, students develop research and collaboration skills, and at the same time obtain a stronger connection with the content. During this process, your goal is to help students improve their critical-thinking skills by asking good questions and challenging them to dig deeper into their topics.

From a teaching perspective, the problem-based activity provides you with the potential to transcend from a textbook-centered learning approach to a more student-centered approach. Your students are actively engaged in carrying out the learning task at hand around their own historical interests.

To maintain engagement and motivation with the problem-based activity, a well-organized lesson is key. Make daily observations to determine if students are on task, working cooperatively, and gaining appropriate understanding around your lesson objectives. To help with this, have your students write a daily journal entry identifying their specific task that day and how their work contributed to the group project as a whole. Collect their journal weekly to provide directed feedback.

At the end of the project, debrief your students by reflecting as a group on the project itself and your students' overall learning process. Ask students what worked with the project and what did not. What would they do differently? What would they add? The feedback can be used to improve your lesson for next time.

Technology tools should be integrated into the project to help students explore, investigate, and understand the problem so that they can begin generating possible solutions. Tools from word processors, spreadsheets, databases, scanners, and digital and video cameras can be incorporated to provide a real-world element to the project.

You can also provide Internet access and telecommunications so students can access relevant and timely information, such as appropriate Web sites, experts in the field, or e-mail to collect personal accounts. Through this process, your students are learning how to use technology to work through a real-world problem.

As your students become more comfortable working through problem-based activities and identifying solutions, encourage them to build on their innovative thought and their ability to move beyond the obvious to a new level of understanding. This innovative thought is what this chapter explores in detail so you can begin creating problem-based activities that will have your students producing creative results.

COGNITIVE ENGAGEMENT

The central goal of problem-based learning is cognitive engagement. The problem should have a central focus in order to create engagement for your students. Meaningful learning requires appropriate engagement.

As a teacher, you have seen your students procedurally engaged, whereby they wait for you to direct and guide their learning. You present the lesson and students take notes. Later, students demonstrate that they understood the material by taking an end-of-unit test.

For students to be *substantially* engaged in the content, you want them to interact with the content in a deep and thoughtful manner. This can be done with a well-designed problem-based activity, such as the newspaper activity described above.

During the project, you move around the room, questioning your students and the groups as a whole, and provide constructive, directed feedback. Throughout this process, your students are learning to become self-reliant by becoming more purposeful in their learning.

Within the problem-based learning project, you want to encourage peer feedback, have students reflect on their own work, and identify specific learning goals that they must carry out throughout the project.

By encouraging students to experiment with their thinking around ideas, allowing them opportunities to learn from mistakes, and developing skills to work through difficult challenges and tasks, you are therefore helping them build upon their ability to reason at a higher level and to become an innovative thinker in the process.

PLANNING FOR PROBLEM-BASED LEARNING

To entice and motivate students to work on a specific problem, such as cleaning up a polluted stream running through their town or to design specific steps that can be taken to save an endangered species, you must have a well-designed problem.

When designing the problem, allow students choice of topic and content of the finished product. This allows them to incorporate their own interests into the activity, thereby allowing them to develop deeper understanding.

Differentiation is also key in this type of activity. All students can be given the same assignment and then each can build on their own understanding and skills. Students will also develop research skills by pulling from a variety of resources, to include personal interviews, video, experiments, books, library databases, and the Internet.

Ask yourself what activity you can incorporate into a lesson that encourages your students to participate in strategic thinking, a form of cognitive effort, and at the same time, motivates them to focus and master the learning task and maintain a high sense of efficacy.

Problem-based learning is a form of systems thinking and design philosophy. It is a process where you want your students to use their prior learning, apply it to the whole system, and then identify multiple relationships with its many distinct parts. Nothing can be focused on in isolation. A holistic view must be taken.

The main tenet of problem-based learning is that your students will produce more self-efficacy in their knowledge construction and as a result have the potential to apply deeper awareness through a range of cognitive meanings. They can then apply these new meanings by transferring them to a deeper context and ultimately to new situations.

COMING UP WITH GOOD IDEAS

In developing a successful problem-based activity, first look at your students, e.g., what are their interests and concerns? Next, identify issues facing your local community or the world as a whole. How does the issue relate to their lives historically and today?

Next, look at your content. What are the major curriculum standards that you want to address? As you identify your standards, begin writing down your goals. What is the "big idea" that you want your students to understand once they complete the lesson?

What methodologies do you want to incorporate into the lesson? Consider the technology available to you and the resources and support.

Consider a challenging problem or task that you would like your students to solve around your identified topic. The problem should be authentic, challenging, and learner centered so that it allows for a full collaborative group effort.

As you think about incorporating a problem-based activity into your classroom, ask yourself the following questions:

- What is the problem?
- What is the current situation of the problem?
- How does the project fit into the overall "big idea" of the subject you are teaching?
- Is there a consequence for your students in solving this problem? In other words, what if your students do research and write an opinion piece in the local newspaper about their findings? Would this be an opportunity or a problem for the school?
- What is the location of the problem? Is it local, national, global?
- What is the intended purpose of completing this project?
- Who is the intended audience?
- How can technology be incorporated?
- Is the project too grand? e.g., is it too much?

- How will you introduce the topic? For example, using a whole-class didactic instruction on the topic and of the proposed project, with a mini-activity or discussion to help introduce the necessary background knowledge.

In designing your problem-based activity, ensure that your students have the necessary background knowledge around the topic being studied. When first beginning this type of activity, short and simple projects to help "get their feet wet" work best. For this initial activity, all students can be working on the same tasks in the same order. As students develop their skills, more autonomy can be provided.

Autonomy can be applied by allowing your students to take more initiative and by defining the scope and goals of their specific part of their project.

Next, set up specific tasks that students will complete, and place these in table format. This *Task Table* can be provided to your students to help guide their learning through the project, keeping them on task, and identifying a specific timeline.

This table will help your students see what needs to be done and will help them break the problem down into manageable parts in order to solve it.

STEP-BY-STEP PROCESS OF PROBLEM SOLVING

There is a distinct, instructional flow that takes place as your students work through a problem. It all begins with the process of exploration. This step requires your students to begin developing cognitive structures, such as identifying specific patterns or relationships that apply to the particular problem.

In this stage, provide students with concrete examples, such as materials they can touch, see, smell, taste, or interact with. At this phase, your role is

Table 8.1.   Task Table

Tasks	Explanation	Resources	Time Estimate	Completed
Task 1				
Task 2				
Subtask 2.1				
Subtask 2.2				

to engage students in questions and comments. Have them share their ideas and overall curiosity with the content. What are they observing? What do they notice? This is where students begin to use their minds to connect to the lesson at hand.

The next step is for students to begin making connections with their prior knowledge by organizing, describing, and discussing with one another what they are noticing and what their specific questions or concerns are. Begin by having students log these connections and concerns by drawing or writing down information and creating a workable draft. Have your students make abstract generalizations to find patterns or formulate rules.

Identify ways that you can get students to think about their own learning. Metacognition should be integrated throughout the problem-based project with activities such as journaling, discussion and self-evaluation, and receiving peer feedback. This provides cognitive activities to help both you and your students determine judgment as well as understanding.

As a teacher, this is also your chance to begin assessing student understanding through formative assessment almost immediately. You want to continually facilitate your students' learning throughout the problem scenario with built-in iterations of information processing.

By observing student acquisition of knowledge and skills obtained with the inclusion of self-reflection and constant monitoring, you can assess the level of interaction with the material and the learning taking place. Notice what words students are using to identify and think about the problem. This will help you determine their level of understanding.

You will also be able to make mental notes on next steps needed to continually engage students and to advance learning within the problem itself.

As the teacher, you want to model good questions for students to ask during this step. Model curiosity and react positively to your students' questions, guiding them to develop even deeper questions. How you interact with your students during each of these stages will determine how engaged they are throughout the problem-based activity process.

Transitioning to the next stage occurs when students begin to explain and revise their understanding. As the teacher, you clarify understanding by building on student descriptions with new information. Pace your content and the skills necessary for students to obtain during this process so students enjoy the challenge and are ready for the next challenge at hand.

During this stage, encourage students' cognitive, physical, and emotional engagement by presenting the material in multiple ways to meet the diverse needs and understanding of your students. Your goal is to ensure that the information is relevant so they want to learn new material.

The next stage is for students to begin sharing the evidence of what they have learned by both analyzing and integrating information, and then applying this information into their new paradigm of understanding. During this stage, provide quality time for students to work with the material and help them publish their findings to demonstrate new knowledge gained in their own words.

Questioning continues during this step. Encourage students to continue questioning both within groups and individually. Encourage students to apply their new knowledge to their own life or the world around them by doing something relevant that will influence change without imitating something someone else has already done, such as what you originally presented.

Have students do something. Write a letter, make a phone call, send an e-mail, interview experts, conduct research on the Internet. Encourage them to be creative to demonstrate their understanding by writing a report, a journal, a letter, preparing an editorial, or role play. They could use animation, a movie, poster, model, or teach what they have learned to others. During this stage, your role is to build on student strengths, thereby enhancing their learning.

The final stage is evaluation. This is where both the student and the teacher reflect on the effectiveness of the lesson. Final questions include:

- What sense did I make of this activity?
- What could I have done differently?
- How do I know that I learned a new skill or have new knowledge?
- How will I use this new information in my everyday life?

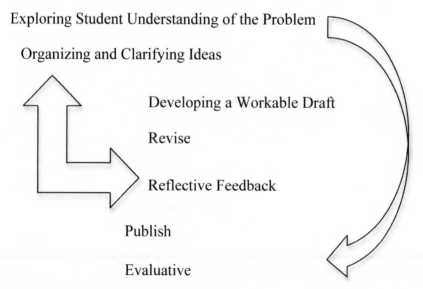

Exploring Student Understanding of the Problem

Organizing and Clarifying Ideas

Developing a Workable Draft

Revise

Reflective Feedback

Publish

Evaluative

Figure 8.1. Step-by-Step Process

PUTTING IDEAS INTO PRACTICE

Designing a problem-based activity that uses the stages described above can be a relatively straightforward task. An example can be illustrated through the following problem-based learning activity regarding government mining of personal data. The goal of this activity is to have students demonstrate knowledge of government, specifically privacy issues and concerns in the 21st century as it relates to the Bill of Rights.

Begin by having students read the Bill of Rights, available at http://www .archives.gov/exhibits/charters/bill_of_rights.html, as well as the history concerning the Bill of Rights, at http://www.archives.gov/exhibits/charters/ constitution_history.html. Hold a discussion on what the students read and have them identify the purpose of the Bill of Rights. Brainstorm how the Bill of Rights protects students and their interests.

Next, have students read government testimony on cyber security and the existing legal framework that is presently protecting privacy in the United States at https://www.cdt.org/testimony/cybersecurity-innovative-solutions -challenging-problems. Other Web resources can be utilized as well.

From there, have students review additional Web resources to gain more knowledge about government searches of personal data using available technology. The "big idea" question for your students becomes: *Is privacy being protected or are the core laws like the Privacy Act presently inadequate in our 21st-century world?*

Now that your students have sufficient background and knowledge on the topic, it is time to present to them the problem:

> You use your debit card to make fast-food purchases weekly on your way to school. Later that week, you go to your primary-care physician for a checkup. About one month later, you get a letter from the U.S. Department of Health and Human Services (DHHS) with a suggestion that you need to make changes to your eating habits.
>
> They provide you with a low-carb, low-fat diet plan designed specifically for you. DHHS suggests that you limit your consumption of fast food. The letter also indicates how many calories and fat you have consumed in fast food over the past month.

Point out to students that based on the scenario presented above, their personal data have been mined. Ask them for their opinion and insight on the government tracking personal information. Present their task of writing a letter regarding this issue to their U.S. government representative.

Have students read about persuasive writing (a sample Web resource can be found at http://www.pbs.org/now/classroom/lessonplan-04.html) so they are informed about how to prepare the document.

Focus their research to tell their congressional representative how they feel about the government's use of data mining, how it relates to the Bill of Rights and new 21st-century issues, and what they think should be done by providing specific examples.

Students face many challenges with this activity. First, they must understand the Bill of Rights and the new concerns that are being raised with this new medium in telecommunications. Second, they need to understand proper correspondence rules such as finding proper addresses, using proper salutations and titles, and remaining factual and appropriate.

Other options for presentation of new knowledge would be to have students create a video or multimedia presentation regarding privacy issues and data mining to help inform their peers.

CHAPTER SUMMARY

Problem-based learning revolves around your curriculum standards and can help your students see the "big picture" of your course. Ensure that enough time is given to research the problem, review one another's work and provide constructive feedback, and use technology tools seamlessly throughout the activity.

Students will develop higher-order thinking skills as they investigate complex problems and work through challenging tasks. The goal of a problem-based learning activity is for each student to make proficient progress toward becoming an independent and creative learner that goes beyond comprehending basic, factual information.

SKILL-BUILDING ACTIVITY

Throughout this chapter we explored how to create a problem-based activity. Looking at your learning standards, identify a good project around a central learning goal in your curriculum. Strive for it to motivate and engage your students. Identify the problem, question, resources, and performance students will complete. Next, prepare an assessment measure and rubric to help guide student understanding.

Chapter Nine

Inquiry and Creativity in Assessments

As you have discovered throughout this book, inquiry revolves around asking good questions about instructional topics in order to encourage students to think critically about the world around them. A follow-up to the inquiry process is the application of effective assessments.

When you incorporate inquiry into your classroom, the goal is to create an interactive activity that engages students in the process of thinking, exploring, and asking informed questions. Thinking is an active process that does not end with the activity, but rather continues through to your assessments culminating from the activity. Your inquiry-oriented activities include assessments that integrate the same creativity and critical-thinking skills you nurtured and developed throughout your activity.

For purposes of this book, assessment is defined as the process of documenting, in measurable terms, knowledge and skills gained from the lesson or activity. Thus, this means that the "big idea" question you identified at the beginning of your lesson and the learning standards that you aligned your question to should be at the center of your activity.

Each inquiry-oriented activity explored throughout this book focuses on creating engaging and directed experiences through the process of discovery. Students are motivated to ask good questions to learn about topics that are outlined by you, the teacher. In conducting assessments to culminate the activity, why not incorporate these same principles into your assessments by tying them into the activity and ultimately into the "big idea" question?

You may be asking how is it possible to tie my "big idea" question and my assessments together to determine student understanding? This chapter lays out a plan of action for you to do just that and to put your assessments at the center of your inquiry-oriented activity.

OVERVIEW

In the classroom, assessments provide an opportunity for learning and feedback for both you and your students. If you keep this line of thought when you develop your assessments, it becomes easier for you to creatively integrate assessments throughout your unit, especially when implementing inquiry-oriented activities.

As teachers, we typically do not think of assessments as learning tools, but instead as dreaded events that happen at the end of a learning unit. Changing this idea and incorporating assessments throughout the unit provides not only a refreshing way to evaluate student progress, but also serves as a tool for you and your students to gauge their understanding of the material.

In identifying your learning standards, you thought about, developed, and then asked your students a "big idea" question to help guide their interests and to ensure they stayed focused on the important concepts to be explored and discovered.

Once you identify your learning standards and the "big idea" question, you recognize ways your students can best demonstrate understanding. From here you move toward identifying strategies for integrating continuous assessments throughout your unit. The effective use of continued assessments ensures that students are on task and are gaining the necessary knowledge based on your learning objectives that you outlined at the beginning of your unit.

To do this, you need to plan your assessments right from the very start of your unit. The idea of planning assessments at the beginning may sound foreign, but think about it. If assessments are viewed as a learning tool, why not incorporate them throughout your unit and begin thinking about assessments at the initial phase in your design stage?

For example, suppose that your next unit is on mathematical fractions. You decide that you want to incorporate a telecollaborative activity into your lesson on fractions to help students discuss important concepts and rules related to fractions as well as to help them identify important real-world use of fractions.

You identify an important standard of learning (SOL) that aligns with the unit on fractions:

- Students will demonstrate knowledge of how to name and write fractions represented by drawings and concrete materials. This activity will also help students understand the difference between the numerator and denominator of a fraction and how to determine each.

Guiding questions could include:

- How can I express fractions verbally, visually, and in writing?
- What questions are important for me to ask about fractions and their relationship to other mathematical concepts I have learned about?
- How do fractions play a role in my everyday world?

Next, determine what key understanding students will gather from the unit. Some possibilities include:

- Key terms such as divisor and numerator.
- Strategies for solving mathematical problems, such as adding, subtracting, and multiplying fractions.
- Analyzing the results for specific problems, numerically and visually.
- General uses of fractions in daily life to help solve real-world problems.

Once you determine what is important for students to understand, choose appropriate assessments in order to evaluate their understanding. Some possibilities to check student progress include:

- Quiz on relevant terms.
- Work on problems related to real-world examples.
- Ask questions about specific problems they encounter in the real world and have students explain their thinking process of solving each.
- Work in small groups to build something, e.g., a bird house, using fractions.
- Have students self-assess by creating blueprints for their product, e.g., birdhouse, design.
- Observe student progress and procedures to determine if they understand.
- Ask higher-order-thinking questions to help students discover new information and to pinpoint possible problems.
- Use "Ask an Expert" to ask questions of math experts and then in large groups reflect on answers.
- Create a Web site to share new understandings of fractions with other students in future classes and in other schools.

Next, you can look at what telecollaborative opportunities are in existence that your students can participate in. Possibilities include:

- Math TV Problem Solving Videos: A telecollaborative project where students learn about mathematical concepts through video creation (available at http://www.mathtv.org/).

- National Math Trail: A telecollaborative project that ties together specific math problems with opportunities to share possible solutions (available at http://www.nationalmathtrail.org/).
- Mathematics Virtual Learning Circle: A project that provides opportunities for students to explore math as it relates to the real world (available at https://media.iearn.org/node/143).
- Connecting Math to Our Lives: A telecollaborative project that ties math into family life (available at http://media.iearn.org/projects/math).

The idea is to use your "big idea" question to help guide your students through the process of learning, in this case, mathematical fractions, as they discover firsthand knowledge about how these broad but interesting concepts relate to their world. At the same time that you are guiding students through the process of learning, you are incorporating meaningful assessments.

This chapter helps guide you through structuring your inquiry activity with continuous assessments in order to determine if students understand the intended learning goals and are achieving the desired results.

FOCUS ON LEARNING AND UNDERSTANDING

Inquiry learning and the different activities that we have explored in this book provide opportunities for student learning through engagement. Part of this engagement comes through continued assessment. Assessments aid *both* teachers and students by helping them determine if the desired results of the lesson are being achieved.

As a teacher, you use many different assessment strategies throughout a lesson to determine if students are gaining the necessary information and to ensure that they can move forward with the lesson. Inquiry-oriented activities are no different.

Assessments take many forms, informally through observations, questioning techniques, small- and large-group work, think-pair-share strategies, and more formally through quizzes and project performances. Other types of assessments include student self-assessments, such as portfolios and learning logs.

The key to an effective assessment strategy is to incorporate assessments throughout your unit to ensure student understanding, not only at the end of a unit through a summative evaluation.

Continued assessment provides opportunities for you as the teacher to determine student performance and understanding of the topics being explored. This provides you with opportunities to guide students and provide feedback to help them get on track if needed or to surge ahead with the activity.

As we learned earlier, Bloom's Taxonomy provides a guide to create activities that encourages students to apply new knowledge and to synthesize this new knowledge by analyzing and asking important questions. To do this successfully, students must understand the broad topics, not just specific tasks and skills. Students then need to apply this broad understanding into a meaningful performance.

An example of a meaningful performance as it relates to an inquiry-oriented activity could be students identifying conflicts and actions within the U.S. Civil War. To get the discussion started, students complete a think-pair-share activity. First, students think about and write down everything they know about the Civil War, including any major events that came before the war.

Paired in small heterogeneous groups, students discuss and share what they wrote down. As a group, they select three events to share with the class which is then documented on the interactive whiteboard. The entire class then groups the events which are saved for later discussion.

This is a form of assessment. This assessment allows the teacher to identify and direct student understanding about the events that led up to the American Civil War. As students identify the main issues of this conflict, the teacher can ask guiding questions to get students to identify misperceptions or to bring in other issues that are being omitted by the students to emphasize specific points.

Assessments provide opportunities for students to tie in prior understanding and personal connections about the topics explored as well as help both students and teachers determine what is understood and what needs further clarification about the topics within the activity.

As the activity continues and students tie their personal interests into what they are learning, you provide opportunities for students to build on their knowledge and to continuously demonstrate their understanding. With each step, you guide students through the process of inquiry using questions and instructional problems as a learning tool. These learning tools are also forms of assessments.

As students build their personal connections around the major goals of the activity, you want your assessments to continue as well. Build on questions, tie in research, and have students continuously share information with their classmates and with you. Entice students to debate with their classmates and possibly with students from outside of the class. Throughout this process you are facilitating the experience in order to ensure that your students are on task, are engaged, and understand what is important.

As students dig deeper and get more involved with the content, they also begin to have a richer experience in terms of more deeply exploring the lesson and discovering new information. Throughout this process, the student and teacher identify benchmarks or performance tasks to ensure that the student is on task. As the teacher, you continually evaluate your students by having them share their findings with others and outline specifically what they learned by discussing and presenting their findings.

The idea of continued assessments is not to wait until the end of an activity to provide feedback to the student, through a summative assessment, but instead to provide measures of performance that involve dynamic and diverse opportunities for reflection and feedback throughout the activity. This helps provide guidance and ensures direction.

IDENTIFYING BENCHMARKS

It is important to identify concrete benchmarks identified from your learning standards and goals. A benchmark is what you want students to understand at specific points in an activity.

For example, you identify a math standard that asks students to explore and manipulate mathematical models in your math class. You want to provide a real-world learning experience so you have students look at seasonal temperatures along a specific latitude and longitude of the atlas.

You find that a Web inquiry activity will work perfectly for this activity and standard. You provide students with an online database, such as http://worldclimate.com. At this Web site, up-to-date information and data are stored on temperatures around the world. Students use this weather database to collect raw data and then, in collaborative groups, they place the data onto a spreadsheet.

Once students place the data in the spreadsheet, the class can convene in a large group to discuss equations to help pull out the necessary data to answer the "big idea" question. As the teacher, you test student understanding of the data collected and the mathematical models needed to solve the necessary problems, such as to predicting temperatures in different geographical regions.

The benchmarks for this example could be placed in several different locations of this activity. One is a brainstorming activity where you ask students about the world map. Next, you can identify and discuss the difference between longitude and latitude and have students hypothesize what the differences mean to weather.

You could introduce climates in various topographies and structures and then question students to interpret and analyze information gathered from the database at the Web site. This allows them to identify the differences and importance of relative and absolute locations and values such as elevation. Another benchmark could be located after students collect the necessary data from the online database.

In small groups, students could outline different mathematical models that could be used to answer questions about the activity. A sample question might be: *What does the height of the sun have to do with earth surface temperature?*

In order for students to get started with this assignment, you need to determine what basic information they need to begin their quest. This involves vocabulary and definition of key terms such as data, average temperature, correlation, regression, and trend lines.

Continuing and expanding this activity, students can be further engaged in discovering relationships between location, physical, and climatic regions along a specific longitude and latitude and then they could consider problems such as population and density, industry, vegetation, and climate. You could also introduce additional Web sites, such as the World Factbook at https://www.cia.gov/library/publications/the-world-factbook/, for students to collect data on items such as population, cities, and topography.

In each of the activities described above, students are actively involved by asking questions and exploring possible answers. You identify where students should be at each point of the activity, and ascertain the answer to the important question which is: *What should students know at this point and how can I identify when and if they know it?*

These benchmarks are shared with your students so they are also aware of what is important. Table 9.1 outlines possible benchmarks for this sample activity.

IDENTIFYING YOUR ESSENTIAL QUESTIONS

When you look at your inquiry activity, ask yourself some questions to help guide you through the design of your unit and to identify what is important for students to understand from the unit itself.

Table 9.1. Benchmarks

Activity	Benchmark
Explore and manipulate a mathematical model that highlights temperature and climate	• Discuss key terms and definitions. • Discuss topography and climate differences. • Identify necessary data from database. • Identify correct mathematical models.

First, to add a real-world element to your unit, ask yourself why it is so important to study this unit anyway. You know your students are thinking this very question, so it is helpful if you can provide a real-world rationale for why this unit is important to them. For example, it is important to understand the basics of mathematical models so that the impact of temperature and ultimately global climates can be determined.

Next, ask yourself what makes this unit universal in scope. In other words, how does it apply to other units and other subject areas? All instructional pieces combine and mix, so ask yourself how your topic combines and mixes with other topics and subjects. For example, what is the connection between mathematical models as they relate to temperature and the topical areas of geography, history, social studies, English, science, and math?

In addition, topics discussed tend to have an underlying issue or problem, so it is important to determine what this is. Identifying the underlying problem helps to grab the interest of your students and it also allows you the opportunity to identify benchmarks and assessment opportunities. One core question you can ask yourself is what would hinder your students if they just did not get it?

As noted earlier, we also want to tie our topics into the bigger picture and relevant, real-world events. How does your topic tie into your students' world? You want to be specific. This ties into why it is important for students to study this particular topic. Figure 9.1 identifies three major questions to help identify essential questions.

IDENTIFYING LEARNING ACTIVITIES

When you look at assessments in the planning stage, focus on your intended outcomes. For example, if your standards state that students must be aware of appropriate nutrition requirements for their weight and age group, then you want them to understand the USDA food pyramid guidelines.

Benchmarks that you can set for this activity would be to have students plan daily diet intakes for different age groups and in different settings. Students could analyze their own eating habits as well as those of family members. A "big idea" question to consider would be: *Why do people eat the way they do?*

Students could be asked to complete specific tasks to ensure understanding of this "big idea" question. For example, they could plan a menu for diverse groups. Or, they could conduct primary research by surveying people, asking them why they eat what they do. You could also have students complete a quiz on the USDA food pyramid to ensure that they understand the basic concepts of food and its relationship to health. Finally, you could have students

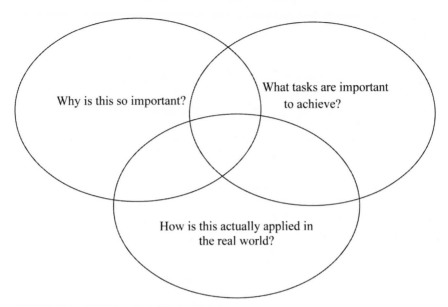

Figure 9.1. Identifying Essential Questions

reflect on their family's eating habits compared to other groups that they have studied thus far in the lesson.

In planning your unit, you want to determine what types of evidence you need to determine if students understand the important concepts of the lesson. For example, try incorporating exercises to increase opportunities for student discovery of specific points and then have them compare and contrast their findings.

Next, ask yourself what specific responses you are looking for to determine if students understand. What determines a correct response or an incorrect response? This is where you create a rubric and criteria to determine student learning. Finally, you want to determine if the evidence that you identified as important actually aligns with your goals and objectives for your unit. Are students learning what you intended?

Questions to consider are:

- What learning activities will strengthen student understanding?
- What performances will highlight student work and align with my learning goals?
- What type of evidence will students need to complete to determine their understanding and strengthen their learning?
- What criteria should be highlighted to determine quality of student work?

- What types of assessments can be utilized to determine who really understood compared to those that only partially understood?

In inquiry-oriented learning, you want students to actively participate and
think about the concepts in the activity like a professional. For example, what
would a historian ask about the American Civil War? What would a scientist
ask about mathematical models?

Students should have the opportunity to use primary-source documents
to compare and contrast and to think critically about topics that impact their
world. Allowing them to conduct primary research enables them to formulate
important questions to help find solutions.

Small teams provide students with opportunities to discuss and debate
issues around topics. Throughout the entire inquiry activity, you can assess
your students through observation, feedback, and performance. You want
them to rehearse and practice tasks, give and receive feedback, and perform
by creating meaningful products.

IDENTIFYING CRITERIA

Identifying criteria that is important for students to accomplish during an
inquiry-oriented activity is an important element to student learning. Rubrics
are a good example of teachers identifying key learning criteria for students
in an activity. Rubrics provide a concise measurement tool to identify what
is important for students to accomplish, and ultimately to understand, about
the activity itself.

When you provide a rubric in the beginning of an activity, you allow students to see what you think is important about the activity. They can work
toward each of the identified criterion in the rubric throughout the activity
itself.

Rubrics are a form of benchmark. They are indicators of understanding.
Rubrics provide students with a score in order for them to determine where
they are in the process. The more intense and specific your rubric is, the more
students know what your expectations are.

It is important to remember that rubrics are only as good as you design
them. The more specific your expectations are and the more your rubric is
aligned with your learning standards, the better your rubric.

For example, if you create a rubric for a lesson on mathematical models,
you have several expectations and criterion to determine what students understood as well as how they performed on each specific task. Table 9.2 provides
an example of a rubric that could be developed for the mathematical model
activity.

Table 9.2. Rubric for Mathematical Models Lesson

Category	Advanced	Proficient	Basic	Below Basic
Students are able to describe and represent mathematical relations using tables.	Data in the table are well organized, accurate, and easy to read.	Data in the table are organized, accurate, and easy to read.	Data in the table are accurate and easy to read.	Data in the table are not accurate and/or cannot be read.
Students are able to describe and represent mathematical relationships using graphs.	The graph is exceptionally well designed, neat, and attractive. A ruler and graph paper (or graphing computer program) were used.	The graph is neat and relatively attractive. A ruler and graph paper (or graphing computer program) were used to make the graph more readable.	Line is neatly drawn but the graph appears quite plain.	The graph appears messy and "thrown together" in a hurry. Line is visibly crooked.
Units on graph.	All units are described (in a key or with labels) and are appropriately sized for the data set.	Most units are described (in a key or with labels) and are appropriately sized for the data set.	All units are not described (in a key or with labels) OR are not appropriately sized for the data set.	Units are neither described NOR appropriately sized for the data set.
Students are able to create rules to explain the relationship between numbers when a change in the first variable affects the second variable.	Rules accurately represent the data and are written in standard form.	Rules accurately represent the data but are not written in standard form.	Rules represent some of the data.	Rules do not represent the data.
Calculation of normal temperature around the globe using a mathematical model.	Uses rules to correctly calculate normal temperature around the globe in degrees Celsius to the nearest tenth.	Uses rules to correctly calculate normal temperature around the globe in degrees Celsius to the nearest degree.	Calculates normal temperature around the globe in degrees Celsius to within 5 degrees.	Does not calculate normal temperature around the globe in degrees Celsius or calculates with an error over 5 degrees.

CHAPTER SUMMARY

Throughout your inquiry-oriented activity, you created a very robust learning experience for your students. You tied experiences into your learning standards and you incorporated real-world elements that ignite student interest and motivation into the process of thinking and ultimately learning.

As you identify learning standards, you also outline your objectives. Next, you outline specifically how students demonstrate understanding throughout the activity. You identify important benchmarks or places within the lesson that provide you and your students with knowledge on how they are doing at that point in the activity. Are they understanding? Do they need guidance to help them move forward?

As benchmarks are identified, you also think about what tasks you want students to complete in order to demonstrate knowledge gained. What performances do you want them to present to confirm understanding? Throughout the activity, you want to ensure that both informal and formal assessments are embedded.

Informal assessments provide opportunities for both you and your students to ask questions to determine if they are on target with what is important in the lesson to understand. Informal assessments include questions as well as observations. Peer feedback and evaluations are also a form of informal assessment. Informal assessments are not intended to be used for a grade, but instead as a measuring tool to determine student understanding.

Formal assessments, in contrast, include quizzes, tests, projects, and activities. As the teacher, you provide feedback on these assessments and allow students to ask questions and develop their understanding. You provide guidance and structure to ensure that students are grasping what is important from the activity.

It is important to provide enough support for students to learn and grow in their understanding of the topics explored. In order to do this, continuous rather than summative assessments are needed. The goal of inquiry-based learning is to ensure that students understand. You do this by tying in real-world experiences and problems, which ultimately increases engagement and understanding of the activity.

In each of the activities explored in this book there have been many opportunities to assess student understanding. In this task you want to ensure that you are not waiting until the end of an activity to evaluate students, but that you identify your criteria early on, share these criteria with your students, and then ensure that they are on task and are understanding the material throughout the activity itself.

CHAPTER REFLECTION

1. Why is continuous assessment important in an inquiry-oriented activity to enhance student learning?
2. Identify three different assessments that you could use to determine if students understand an important topic within an inquiry-oriented activity?
3. Why are benchmarks important when planning for assessments within an inquiry-oriented activity?
4. How do rubrics improve student learning in an inquiry-oriented activity?

SKILL-BUILDING ACTIVITY

This activity focuses on incorporating continuous assessments throughout your inquiry-oriented activity. Revisit an inquiry-oriented activity and review your learning standards, topics, and resources. Write down four specific benchmarks you want your students to achieve. Next, determine what activities will help students meet each of these benchmarks. Write down each activity, highlighting SOLs for each one. Design and develop a rubric that aligns with your identified SOLs and identify specific criteria. Ask a colleague to review your benchmarks, rubric, and standards, and provide feedback. Are your learning assessments meaningful? Do they align with your standards? Is your rubric helpful and accurate?

Chapter Ten

Inquiry in Education Using Technology

Throughout the activities explored in this text, inquiry has been continually emphasized and stressed. Technology is used as a tool to engage students in the process of learning as well as to provide a real-world element to the lesson.

In a lesson that integrates technology, the technology itself does not take the lead role but rather is used to communicate, analyze, and present information. This chapter further explores and expands upon the integration of technology as a tool to further engage your students in inquiry.

OVERVIEW

Technology tools and the Internet have the potential to enhance lessons in a classroom, but when the tools also encourage inquiry, then student engagement can increase even more. As an example, see the Peace Corps World Wise Schools Web site at http://wws.peacecorps.gov/wws/. This Web site was created for teachers to integrate cross-cultural lessons, stories, activities, and videos into their classrooms to engage students in conversation about different cultures and service learning.

Within the Web site, students are able to read letters, see videos, and listen to podcasts from Peace Corp volunteers about their field experiences. When you incorporate these technology tools into your classroom instruction and allow your students instant access to these real-world expeditions, your students become more engaged and are able to ask meaningful questions about culture, language, and global society.

This chapter highlights how technology can be integrated into your inquiry unit to engage students to ask essential questions in order to dig deeper into issues that surround us as a global society. Questions regarding war and peace, gender and race equality, global warming, homelessness, healthcare, and education equity are major societal issues that can be presented to students.

Students can formulate questions and you can then help them explore results using technology tools and an integrated technology lesson plan. In so doing, you are tying in your standards of learning revolving around your course topics of math, science, history, language, etc.

SUPPORTING CURRICULAR GOALS WITH TECHNOLOGY

Any technology tool that is used in the classroom to engage students in inquiry must emphasize curriculum goals. Technology tools are best utilized in a classroom when they enhance active engagement of the learner, utilize collaborative groups, encourage feedback and interaction, and provide connection to experts in the field of study.

In this 21st century, technology touches many aspects of our everyday world. We communicate via the Internet, receive data from satellites, and record progress through digital images. Technology in the classroom has the potential to provide students with experiences that they will encounter in the world of work or in their everyday lives. Having students interact with technology provides an element of meaning, relevancy, and application to the lesson.

Technology integration means more than teaching students how to use a word processor. Integrating technology successfully into a lesson means using the Internet, digital cameras, and software applications as a transparent tool that engages your students.

Inquiry-oriented activities can help provide students with meaningful classroom lessons and activities by having them work with diverse, relevant, and interesting data as well as provide students with opportunities to express themselves through images, sound, and text.

Technology tools are best integrated when they are student driven. For example, students gather relevant and timely data, aid in analyzing and synthesizing those data, and later present the data in meaningful ways to the rest of the class. In an inquiry-oriented activity, technology tools can help teachers offer students the ability to:

- Access relevant data in a timely manner, such as through the use of primary-source documents.
- Collect and record information, such as through the use of an Internet database or spreadsheet.

- Collaborate with experts and other students around the world, such as by asking an expert and e-pals (see http://www.epals.com/).
- Present information through multimedia, such as with the use of images, sound, and/or text.
- Have meaningful and authentic assessments, such as real-world problems and projects.
- Present new student knowledge to the world for review and feedback.

MEANINGFUL LEARNING

When adjusting your lessons to an inquiry approach to teaching and learning, try to move away from using technology solely to deliver content. Instead, seamless technology integration becomes the link to creating engaging inquiry-oriented activities that would be impossible to achieve without integrating technology tools. Table 10.1 provides an outline of moving up Bloom's Taxonomy using technology integration as a tool.

INSTRUCTIONAL TECHNOLOGY TOOLS

Technology tools can be accessed directly from your computer, such as a Web browser or a word processing program. Or they can be accessed and manipulated directly on the Internet, such as an image editing or video editing program. Determine what types of tools you have available and which tools will allow students to explore the "big idea" question you identified for them in order to gain the essential understanding of your content.

One way to select appropriate technology for each of your learning tasks is to consider the following:

- What types of learners are your students? Are they visual, verbal, musical, kinesthetic, interpersonal, intrapersonal, logical, naturalist, and/or existential?
- What are your learning objectives?
- From past lessons, what did your students not understand?
- What technology tool(s) do you have available to you?

For example, in a literature lesson you want students to understand that literature mirrors life, language, and culture. In the past, you had students read a literary work, discuss major themes, and then write a paper on these major themes. At the end of the unit, you found that your students were unable to connect the themes and could not relate the themes to real-life events or ideas.

Table 10.1. Bloom's Taxonomy and Technology Integration

Bloom's Taxonomy:	Remember	Understand	Apply	Analyze
Engage	• Recognize • List • Describe • Name • Locate	• Interpret • Summarize • Infer • Paraphrase • Compare • Explain	• Implement • Use information • Execute tasks	• Compare • Organize • Structure • Integrate
Collaborate	• Presentation given by the teacher on a topic. • Bookmarking a Web page for future use.	• Journal using a blog with a focus on writing a task-specific entry.	• Students choose a software program or operate and manipulate hardware and software applications. • Students apply new knowledge to tasks.	• Students create mashups where several data sources are combined into a single set of usable information to create meaning, such as in GoogleLitTrips.
Constructivist	• Use a social bookmarking tool, such as Delicious, to store Web sites for the class to access from any computer with an Internet connection.	• Use a microblog, such as Twitter, to write brief entries sharing information with group members.	• Share and manipulate content on shared networks, such as Flickr or wikis.	• Students connect information through links within documents and Web pages in order to clarify, analyze, and synthesize content.

Authentic	• Conduct a key word search using only keywords or terms.	• Categorize, comment, and annotate Web pages.	• Add, remove, and alter content on Web sites in order to add to the body of knowledge, such as Wikipedia.	• Compare and contrast information. • Question information and lead discussions on information from experts in the field. • Reflect on learning through blogging and participate on experts' blogs.
Standards	• Teachers set learning goals. • Teachers use technology as delivery devices. • Teachers use the tool in a basic way.	• Activities are monitored by the teacher. • Results are evaluated with some reflection from students. • Some integration of technology; goes beyond simple drill and practice.	• More student centered activities. • Incorporate more metacognition from the student that would not be available without technology tools.	• Students take control of their own learning. • Students become active participants by identifying prior knowledge and new understanding. • Students ask deeper questions of content and determine what is important.

To address these issues, you research the possibility of creating an inquiry-oriented activity and integrating technology into your lesson. Your goal is to engage students into the major themes of the literary works you are going to read throughout the semester. You also want them to share their understanding with others in a global context. See Table 10.2 below for an example.

As you conduct your research, you discover GoogleLitTrips at http://googlelittrips.com, a virtual world that allows students to study and explore literature through the creation of maps that incorporate multimedia elements. This map with the inclusion of the multimedia elements is called a mashup and allows your students to add place marks on Google Maps that can contain video, sound, images, hyperlinks, and/or text.

Table 10.2. Identifying Technology Tools

Student Needs
- Visual
- Verbal
- Musical
- Kinesthetic
- Interpersonal
- Logical
- Naturalist, and/or
- Existential

Learning Objective:
- Study two characters in the reading.
- Evaluate each character and compare these figures' accomplishments and setbacks.
- Design an appropriate presentation that includes video, sound, and text to tell the characters' story.

What did students not understand from past lessons?
- An ability to analyze and synthesize information from literary works.
- The ability to relate the literary works to major themes and issues of the authors' era as well as society at large.

Technology Tools Utilized
- Students read and then discuss literary themes in a class discussion and then share their thoughts and analysis about the discussion on a classroom blog.
- Students work in small groups to research specific characters and places within the story.
- The research consists of gathering primary source data, such as images, sound files, video, and Web resources, to highlight student understanding of the characters.
- Students then have opportunities to create artifacts such as video, sound files, Internet resources, and text and to incorporate these into their presentation.
- Students combine the multimedia elements and place on GoogleMaps in order to share with the GoogleLitTrips global audience.

21ST-CENTURY SKILLS

As you think about your inquiry-oriented activity and how best to integrate technology tools, it is important to include 21st-century skills, such as communication, managing projects, and using technology, as well as the National Educational Technology Standards for Students (NET-S) developed by the International Society of Technology Education (ISTE).

By incorporating inquiry-oriented learning into your lessons, you move beyond basic subject or content mastery to more sophisticated thinking about real-world skills and ideas. As discussed earlier, inquiry-oriented activities allow students to use higher-order thinking skills, such as analysis, evaluating, and creating.

It also follows then that it is important to utilize rubrics as an assessment tool to guide your students and focus them on what is important to understand about the inquiry-oriented activity.

The National Education Standards for Students (NET-S) provides standards of integrating technology tools into teaching and learning to enhance the following student skills:

- Creativity and innovation, such as developing innovative products and processes.
- Communication and collaboration, such as using technology tools to support learning.
- Research and information fluency, such as using technology tools to gather, evaluate, and utilize information.
- Critical thinking, problem solving, and decision making, as well as the ability to analyze and synthesize new knowledge.

Table 10.3. Higher Order Thinking

Higher Order Thinking and Bloom's Taxonomy	
Analyze	• Explain
	• Classify
	• Investigate
	• Illustrate
Evaluate	• Justify
	• Debate
	• Recommend
	• Decide
Create	• Combine
	• Invent
	• Design
	• Compose

- Digital citizenship, such as an understanding of ethical uses of technology and equity issues.
- Technology operations and concepts, to include understanding the language, systems, and operations of technology tools.

As you design your inquiry-oriented activity, you additionally identify how you want students to demonstrate their understanding of the major concepts and themes they are exploring.

Ask yourself the following questions:

- Can technology provide a medium for students to express themselves and share their new knowledge with others in a meaningful way?
- What will students be able to do or know once they finish this inquiry activity, and how can they share it with others?
- How can you integrate real-world examples or artifacts into the inquiry-oriented activity to engage students and to get them to think and explore the bigger picture?
- How can technology enhance these examples, such as incorporating ideas or discussions of experts in the field, into your classroom by using a resource such as ePals or a Web log (blog)?

CHAPTER SUMMARY

The critical takeaway from this chapter discussion is the importance of using technology tools that help students achieve their learning goals. The implementation of real-world authentic inquiry-oriented activities into your classroom means integrating technology tools seamlessly in ways that are meaningful and provide real-world application. When designing inquiry-oriented activities, your goal is to create instructional tasks that have students finding, evaluating, and synthesizing information from a variety of sources.

Some source examples include the American Memory Project at the Library of Congress, available at http://memory.loc.gov/, to gather primary-source artifacts or a database at the U.S. Fish and Wildlife Organization at http://www.fws.gov/refuges/databases/tes.html to collect data on endangered species by habitat. The possibilities are endless.

CHAPTER REFLECTION

1. Identify learning objectives that emphasize Bloom's Taxonomy.
2. How does your inquiry activity emphasize 21st-century skills?

3. Determine how you can integrate technology into your inquiry-oriented lesson to highlight collaboration and communication skills.

SKILL-BUILDING ACTIVITY

Throughout chapter ten, inquiry and how technology can be integrated with inquiry activities in order to provide meaningful, real-world experiences to students was explored. The idea of an inquiry-oriented activity is to engage students with a "big idea" question and provide learning activities that engage them in discovery and investigation. In order for students to be properly engaged, you want to highlight the higher-order thinking skills of analysis, evaluation, and creativity. Your goal at the conclusion of this chapter is to find ways to effectively integrate technology tools with your learning objectives and emphasize real-world skills.

Chapter Eleven

Learning at a Distance

In K–12, distance learning is growing in popularity among schools, teachers, and students alike. Distance learning takes many forms. It can be a Web-enhanced class, a flipped classroom, or a course with instruction completely delivered online. Simply put, distance learning is when you deliver instruction and course content through the Internet using Web-based methods.

These methods can include video, audio, print-based, multimedia, or text. Online instruction and learning at a distance can help meet the needs of students by providing them with pedagogical options. It can also allow for deeper access to materials and resources.

This chapter explores distance learning and how you can use this approach to teaching as an enhancement to the classroom or to deliver instruction completely online.

OVERVIEW

Around the United States, virtual K–12 schools are being created. Some are designed to provide credit-recovery courses to students and some focus on the home schooled. In addition, the local school systems are also discovering the benefits of offering distance-learning courses. As a result, they too are beginning to provide online learning for both credit recovery and advanced coursework.

When offering learning at a distance and teaching online, it is necessary to rethink your teaching practice. The traditional pedagogical practices used in a face-to-face classroom need to be adapted to the online environment. Learning materials are revamped or extended so that they are visible and easily accessible. Copyright issues and other ethical considerations need to be taken into account.

Specific teaching strategies and instructional practices must also be analyzed. You are creating a learning environment that builds on the principles of community and collaboration. Interaction should be incorporated and encouraged. Interactive strategies include student coaching, guided practice, and group collaboration.

Interactive course design requires students to be actively engaged with the content, whether it is participating with a simulation, watching a video and answering questions, or peer editing. In an online course, you are designing ways for students to work with others, actively engage with the material to strengthen prior understanding, and gain new knowledge.

GETTING STARTED

To prepare and plan for instruction from a distance, it is helpful to look at three theories developed and supported by Gagne (1995), Keller (1987), and Bloom (1984).

GAGNE'S NINE EVENTS OF INSTRUCTION

In his research, Gagne (1995) identified an instructional model that allows teachers to design course content around the learner from an instructional context. He suggested nine interrelated events of instruction that must occur before learning can take place.

The first event is to gain student attention. When students are attentive, they are focused on learning and the activity. Gaining attention can be done through an introductory quote, video, illustration, cartoon, or even an audio file. It should be interesting and relate to the content. It should encourage and motivate students to seek deeper knowledge.

In Gagne's second event, students are informed clearly and concisely about the learning objectives for the lesson. The learning goal is communicated and

Gain Attention > Learning Objectives > Prior Knowledge > Stimulus >

Structure & Guidance > Practice > Feedback > Evaluation > Transfer

Figure 11.1. Gagne's Nine Events of Instruction

students understand why it is important. Visuals or auditory tools can be used to communicate these items: for example, an audio file, a text file, a concept map, or an illustration.

In the third event, the prior knowledge of students is called upon by reminding them of past learning activities and how these past experiences are relevant to this new activity. Learning happens as a continuum and students become aware that they are building on their knowledge piece by piece. Ask questions about specific facts, procedures, rules, or vocabulary words that students learned in a previous lesson. Ensure that they can apply this former knowledge to the new lesson.

In the fourth event, you present a specific stimulus or material that you want students to learn. This is the main idea of your lesson, which you want students to grasp and understand when they complete your identified task.

Apportion the stimulus into manageable "chunks" and sequence the information so that it is clear and builds on each element systematically. Present the stimulus through images, text, simulations, watching a video, or listening to an expert.

The fifth event involves providing structure and guidance. Even if your lesson is student-centered, structure is necessary. Incorporate strategies for students to complete the task successfully. Provide a handout with specific guidelines and instructions to help students move through the steps for successful completion of the activity.

Practice is the sixth identified event. Students need to practice their new skill to make sure they are able to perform the task in new ways. A hands-on activity is best to allow students to run through the newly acquired knowledge or skill. Through practice, they will remember and understand what they are learning because they build connections between the activity and the content.

Receiving constructive feedback from you and classmates is the seventh instructional event identified by Gagne. By providing feedback, you help students reorganize misinformation and strengthen accurate information. This can be done either orally or in writing.

The eighth event is the evaluation event. This is important because it lets you and your students know specifically about their performance. How did they do? What did they understand? This step provides information on what was learned during the lesson.

The ninth and final event is to enhance student retention and transfer of knowledge gained. If students are given a similar situation or problem, will they be able to solve the problem? Do they need additional practice and feedback? If they can solve the problem, then it was a job well done. If not, review key areas for knowledge retention.

Additionally, you want to ensure that students transfer lessons learned. Can students build on their learning and transfer it to a new situation?

Gagne's nine events are closely tied to the cognitive sciences and brain research. Gagne believes that each of these events is essential to incorporate into a lesson for learning to take place.

As a teacher supporting Gagne's theory and teaching at a distance, you want to design online instruction by selecting appropriate media and materials, strategies, and methods, and creating a learning environment that supports each of these nine events.

KELLER'S ARCS MOTIVATION MODEL

Another equally important model was created by Keller (1987). He examined designing instruction with motivational facets integrated into activities to engage students in the learning process. Maintaining student interest and motivation is critical when students are learning at a distance.

Keller identified four elements:

- attention
- relevance
- confidence building
- a supportive classroom climate

Maintaining curiosity or attention is necessary to keep students focused throughout the lesson. One of the best ways to accomplish this is through engagement in a real-world task.

Learning and relevance of content go hand in hand. It is important to find ways to relate to student interests and needs. Students learn best and remember longer when the content is relevant.

Throughout the learning activity, build confidence in your students by providing appropriate learning materials as well as a supportive and receptive classroom climate. All students should be able to freely ask questions, provide and receive support, and grow as learners.

Keller's model builds on student confidence by designing instruction that is manageable for each student. Build in opportunities for students to be successful and to have a sense of personal control throughout the learning activity. Provide opportunities for students to obtain intrinsic reinforcement as you provide extrinsic rewards and maintain equity throughout the lesson.

The overall premise of Keller's ARCS model is to increase student motivation by providing perceptual and inquiry arousal, as well as a sense of variability in instruction to help build and maintain attention and interest. Keller's model also ensures that the lesson is goal oriented and matches student motives by building on the familiar.

In both Gagne's and Keller's models, student-centered and relevant instruction are at the core of each instructional process. In each, a learning environment is created that provides organization and clearly defined learning goals that are obtainable for students in a successful lesson.

Throughout this book, we have focused on the importance of creating student-centered, inquiry-oriented learning environments that are both relevant for your students and engaging. Designing an online course is no different.

BLOOM'S TAXONOMY

Bloom's (1984) Taxonomy is a third model that assists in designing instruction to meet student needs. As we discussed earlier in the text, Bloom created a taxonomy to help classify instructional tasks that a learner works through in order to move to a higher level of critical thinking and creativity. His taxonomy begins with rote learning and comprehension and moves up the levels to complex thinking, application, analysis, synthesis, and finally evaluation.

While students need to understand content and facts, this is not a learning level where you want students to remain. A goal should be to move students to the upper levels of Bloom's Taxonomy, e.g., creating ideas and thinking in new and innovative ways.

In considering each of the above three models and designing your online course, consider what your enduring questions should be. Focus on the "big idea" question that you want your students to grasp. Next, what are the essential questions within the content that you want students to understand? If you approach your online course design in this manner, you will be able to successfully apply the ideas of Gagne, Keller, and Bloom and incorporate their models into your online lessons.

As an example, suppose that you are teaching a literature lesson. The ultimate goal or learning outcome would be that students realize that literature deals with universal themes and these themes can be applied to everyday lives. Thus, your essential "big idea" question would be: *How are universal themes expressed in literature?*

This "big idea" question helps to provide focus in designing the lesson. The intent is to grab student attention and build engagement. In the online course, a discussion could be created that has students brainstorm about this question and how it applies to their readings.

Various literature texts could be reviewed, such as *To Kill a Mockingbird*, and students could list themes encountered in the various books. Students would critically examine the various themes and begin relating them to their life and the world around them.

TECHNOLOGY AND DISTANCE LEARNING

Technology and distance learning work well together. When thinking about technology and instruction, think about ways you integrate technology into your daily life. Do not start with the technology tool, rather first start with your teaching goal. Then think about how the technology tool will help achieve that goal successfully.

For example, you are planning a trip and you want to know the quickest route. You access the Internet and go to MapQuest at http://www.mapquest .com. You type in your beginning and final addresses, and receive driving directions. This is an efficient and effective use of technology. When thinking about technology integration in your online course, think of it in the same way as this real-world application.

As with any new learning environment, try to anticipate the learning curve that your students will experience when learning at a distance or using a Web-enhanced delivery of instruction. To help students be successful and effective, provide them with sufficient time within the course to become familiar with the materials. Encourage them to ask questions both to you and to each other.

Scaffolding and "chunking" your information can also help students understand the material and how it is presented. Provide assistants or avatars throughout the course to guide them with specific instruction to build skills.

Sequencing is also key. Plan how students should most effectively move through the content, progressing and building on their overall knowledge. Provide a clear outline that advances students through the learning objectives.

Learning at a distance can enhance a student's 21st-century skills. Just as in the face-to-face classroom, students are being asked to be creative and inventive thinkers. With the use of the Web, they are also developing digital literacy, communication skills, and the ability to use a variety of computer tools.

To build these 21st-century skills in an online environment, think about how students can work with the content to build connections, such as through threaded discussions, using Web resources to gather data, and manipulating and presenting information in new and different ways. How can meaningful connections be created between the content and the technology tool to help enhance the information for your students and ultimately help them learn?

LITERACY INSTRUCTION

As we discussed in chapter three with information literacy, we now live in a global economy and our focus is on education with 21st-century skill development.

How can you incorporate appropriate technologies into literacy instruction to engage students around broad themes? Simply put, what will allow your students to read, think, write, and speak to practice necessary literacy skills?

Going back to constructivist principles of learning, where a learning environment is created that is student centered, with each activity built on the main pillar, students must construct their own understanding in an active or participatory manner through social interactions and small-group work.

"Chunk" and sequence the content for your learner. When you provide snippets of information and appropriate interaction with the content and one another, your students will be able to stay focused and maintain interest throughout the process.

Consider multiple ways students can work with the material. By providing students with multiple ways to learn content in specific and structured ways that are meaningful to them, you improve the success of your students in a Web-enhanced or totally online environment.

DIFFERENTIATION

When incorporating distance learning, accessibility to the content needs some consideration. There are basic guidelines, which we discussed above, such as not presenting information in only one way, the use of tables or videos so that they can be read by screen readers, etc.

The National Center for Accessible Media works with organizations to ensure that content offered online is accessible for all learners. They provide a list of resources to help deliver and design online content. See http://ncam .wgbh.org/invent_build/web_multimedia/tools-guidelines.

Explicit instructions are important to incorporate into lessons for students with learning disabilities. The need to break down complex activities into manageable chunks and sequenced steps is necessary. Providing think sheets or note-taking guides for students to utilize throughout the lesson can also be helpful.

Throughout this book, we have highlighted the need for authentic tasks. Learning at a distance is no different. Learning occurs when students can associate the material and content to their personal understanding and interests. Using simulations and real-world problems will aid in this important goal.

The basic universal design for learning is to provide multiple means for learners to acquire the necessary content, allow students to express understanding of the lesson in multiple ways, and increase student motivation so that they can engage with the content through exploring personal interests.

Table 11.1. Presenting Your Online Content

Multiple Ways to Present Your Online Content	
Multiple Representations	Video, audio, slide shows, various reading levels, variety of support resources, translations, graphic representations such as diagrams, images, and illustrations. Reading material at various difficulty levels.
Multiple Ways to Express Understanding	Writing, audio, maps, diagrams, videos, slide shows, graphs, concept maps, outlines, hands-on activities, blogs, wikis, shared writing or editing.
Multiple Ways for Engagement	Role playing, interview experts, threaded discussions, brainstorming, working with teams, experiments, playing games, community involvement in an issue.

CHAPTER SUMMARY

This chapter provided an overview of learning at a distance from an inquiry perspective. It examined various strategies and methods that can be incorporated into an online learning environment.

CHAPTER REFLECTION

1. In what ways should teaching at a distance mirror face-to-face teaching?
2. What specific methods and strategies can be used to tailor content for individual needs of learners at a distance?
3. How can quality instruction be adhered to at a distance?

SKILL-BUILDING ACTIVITY

Throughout this chapter, we explored how to create a lesson that incorporates distance learning into a student-centered environment while working on an authentic task. Your task is to plan an online activity that will require your students to collaborate with others to build a specific skill or understanding around a learning objective. As you think about your activity, incorporate the elements below:

- Identify a real-world problem your students will need to solve in a collaborative group.
- Identify how you will provide multiple representations of content in an online setting.
- Identify ways in which your students will demonstrate their understanding in multiple ways through the Web.
- Identify a technology tool that you can use to motivate students and gain their attention. Describe how this tool aligns with your learning objective.
- Provide methods for your students to read, write, and reflect on their new understanding within an online group discussion forum.

References

CHAPTER 1: WHAT IS INQUIRY?

Bloom, B., Englehart, M., Furst, E., Hill, W., & Krathwohl, D. (1956). *Taxonomy of educational objectives: The classification of educational goals. Handbook I: The cognitive domain.* New York: David McKay.

Bransford, J., Brown, A., & Cocking, R. (eds.). (1999). *How people learn.* National Research Council, Washington, DC: National Academy Press. Retrieved from http://www.nap.edu/openbook/0309065577/html/index.html

Center for Innovation in Engineering and Science Education. Retrieved from http://www.ciese.org/collabprojs.html

Connect to the Classroom: Inquiry-based Learning. Retrieved from http://www.thirteen.org/edonline/concept2class/inquiry/index.html

Exploratorium: The Museum of Science, Art and Human Perception at the Palace of Fine Arts. Retrieved from http://www.exploratorium.edu/

Integration: Building 21st Century Learning Environments. Retrieved from http://www.landmark-project.com/edtechnot_warlick/

Krathwohl, D. R., Bloom, B. S., & Masia, B. B. (1973). *Taxonomy of educational objectives, the classification of educational goals, Handbook II: The affective domain.* New York: David McKay.

Learning for the 21st Century. Retrieved from http://21stcenturyskills.org/downloads/P21_Report.pdf

YouthLearn: An Introduction to Inquiry-based Learning. Retrieved from http://www.youthlearn.org/learning/general-info/our-approach/intro-inquiry-learning/intro-inquiry-learning

CHAPTER 2: DESIGNING
INSTRUCTION FOR CREATIVE THINKING

Anderson, L., & Krathwohl, D. (eds.). (2001). *A taxonomy for learning, teaching, and assessing: A revision of Bloom's taxonomy of educational objectives.* Boston: Allyn & Bacon.

Bloom, B., Englehart, M., Furst, E., Hill, W., & Krathwohl, D. (1956). *Taxonomy of educational objectives: The classification of educational goals. Handbook I: The cognitive domain.* New York: David McKay.

Gardner, H. (2009). *5 minds for the future.* North Ryde, Sydney: McGraw-Hill.

Google Documents. Retrieved from http://www.google.com/google-d-s/documents/

GoogleSketchUp. Retrieved from http://sketchup.google.com/

Interactive Tour of the Civil Rights Museum. Retrieved from http://www.civilrights museum.org/

Kim, K. H. (2011). The creativity crisis: The decrease in creative thinking scores on the Torrance tests of creative thinking. *Creativity Research Journal, (23)*4.

Marzano, R., Pickering, D., & Pollock, J. (2001). *Classroom instruction that works.* Alexandria, VA: Association for Supervision and Curriculum Development.

Merriam-Webster Online Dictionary. Retrieved from http://www.merriam-webster .com

Petra, T. J. (n.d.). Real World Math.org. Concept Lessons: Volume of Solids. Retrieved from http://www.realworldmath.org/concept-lessons.html

Project Budburst Database. Retrieved from http://neoninc.org/budburst

Real World Math. Retrieved from http://www.realworldmath.org

Robinson, K. (2010, October). TED Video: Changing Education Paradigms. Retrieved from http://youtube/mCbdS4hSa0s

Terman, L. M., & Oden, M. H. (1959). *The gifted group at mid-life: Thirty-five years follow-up of the superior child.* Stanford, CA: Stanford University Press.

U.S. Climate Map. Retrieved from http://www.ncdc.noaa.gov/oa/climate/research/ cag3/cag3.html

VoiceThread. Retrieved from http://voicethread.com

CHAPTER 3: EMBEDDING
INFORMATION LITERACY INTO YOUR COURSE

ABCs of Web Site Evaluation. Retrieved from http://kathyschrock.net/abceval/

All about Explorers—Christopher Columbus. Retrieved from http://allaboutexplorers .com/explorers/columbus/

Christopher Columbus Biography. Retrieved from http://www.biography.com/ people/christopher-columbus-9254209/

Dihydrogen Monoxide Research Division. Retrieved from http://www.dhmo.org/

Gardner, H. (2009). *5 minds for the future.* North Ryde, Sydney: McGraw-Hill.

Georgia O'Keeffe Museum. Retrieved from http://www.okeeffemuseum.org/art -exhibitions.html

Intentionally Misleading Web Sites. Retrieved from http://www.techlearning.com/ article/intentionally-misleading-web-sites/42539

Kathy Schrock's Critical Evaluation Surveys. Retrieved from http://www.schrock guide.net/critical-evaluation.html

National Association of Clean Air Agencies. Retrieved from http://www.4cleanair .org/

National Weather Service. Retrieved from http://www.nws.noaa.gov

Need Help, How to Spot a Fake. Retrieved from http://report-online-scams.com/how -to-spot-a-fake-website/

News of the Weird. Retrieved from http://www.newsoftheweird.com/

Teacher Tap: Evaluating Internet Resources. Retrieved from http://eduscapes.com/ tap/topic32.htm

Urban Legends. Retrieved from http://urbanlegends.about.com/

CHAPTER 4: SETTING UP AN ACTIVITY: TYING GOOD QUESTIONS TO OBJECTIVES

Authentic Education: Big Ideas. Retrieved from http://www.authenticeducation.org/ ae_bigideas/index.lasso

Bloom, B. S. (1984). *Taxonomy of educational objectives*. Boston: Allyn & Bacon.

From Now On: Promoting Thinking and the Growth of Thinkers. Retrieved from http://fnopress.com/pedagogy/modules/toc.htm

From Now On: The Question is the Answer. Retrieved from http://fno.org/oct97/ question.html

Goetz, E., Alexander, P., & Ash, M. (1992). Understanding and enhancing students' cognitive processes. In *Educational psychology: A classroom perspective*. New York: Merrill.

CHAPTER 5: CREATING A WEBQUEST

A Rubric for Evaluating WebQuests. Retrieved from http://WebQuest.sdsu.edu/Web Questrubric.html

Filimentality Web-based Activity Tool. Retrieved from http://www.kn.att.com/wired/ fil/

Process Guides: Student Guides. Retrieved from http://projects.edtech.sandi.net/ staffdev/tpss99/processguides/index.htm

Teachnology: WebQuest Generator. Retrieved from http://www.teach-nology.com/ web_tools/web_quest/

WebQuest .org. Retrieved from http://WebQuest.org/index.php

CHAPTER 6: CREATING A WEB INQUIRY ACTIVITY

Inquiry Page: Learning Begins with Questions. Retrieved from http://www.cii .illinois.edu/InquiryPage/

Library of Congress: American Memory Project. Retrieved from http://memory.loc .gov

U.S. Census Bureau: State Facts for Students. Retrieved from http://www.census.gov/ schools/facts/

U.S. Department of Labor: Student Page. Retrieved from http://www.dol.gov/dol/ audience/aud-students.htm

Web Inquiry Projects. Retrieved from http://webinquiry.org/

YouthLearn: How to Create an Inquiry-based Project. Retrieved from http://www .youthlearn.org/learning/planning/lesson-planning/how-inquiry/how-inquiry

CHAPTER 7: CREATING A TELECOLLABORATIVE ACTIVITY

Ask an Expert. Retrieved from http://www.ask.com

Collaborative Learning Center at GlobalSchoolNet.org. Retrieved from http://www .globalschoolnet.org/gsncenter/

Connect Teleprojects. Retrieved from http://exchange.co-nect.net/Teleprojects/

ePals Global Community. Retrieved from http://www.epals.com/

Global Grocery List Project. Retrieved from http://landmark-project.com/ggl/index .html

Global SchoolNet. Retrieved from http://www.globalschoolnet.org/index.cfm

GLOBE Program. Retrieved from http://www.globe.gov/

Harris, J. (1995, April). Mining the Internet column. *The Computing Teacher*, *22*(7). Retrieved from http://lrs.ed.uiuc.edu/Mining/April95-TCT.html

Harris, J. (2001, May). Teachers as telecollaborative project designers: A curriculum-based approach. *Contemporary Issues in Technology and Teacher Education, 1*(3), 429–42. Retrieved from http://www.citejournal.org/vol1/iss3/seminal/article1.htm

iEARN Collaboration Centre: Projects. Retrieved from https://media.iearn.org/ projects

International Education and Resource Network (iEARN). Retrieved from http://www .iearn.org/

International Telementor Program. Retrieved from http://www.telementor.org/

KidLink. Retrieved from http://www.kidlink.org/

KidLink Project Center. Retrieved from http://www.kidlink.org/drupal/project/

Library of Congress: American Memory Project. Retrieved from http://memory.loc .gov

Mad Sci Network. Retrieved from http://www.madsci.org

TEAMS Educational Resources: A Resource Page Provided by the Los Angeles County Office of Education. Retrieved from http://teams.lacoe.edu/documentation/ projects/projects.html

Telecollaborative Learning Project examples. Retrieved from http://www.2learn.ca/
United Nations: Global Classroom. Retrieved from http://www.unausa.org/global
-classrooms-model-un
Virtual Architecture's Web. Retrieved from http://virtual-architecture.wm.edu/index
.html

CHAPTER 8: CREATING A PROBLEM-BASED ACTIVITY

Garner, B. K. (2008).*Getting to got it!: Helping struggling students learn how to
learn*. Alexandria, VA: Association for Supervision and Curriculum Development.
Harris, L. (2011, May 25). *Cybersecurity: Innovative solutions to challenging problems*. Center for Democracy and Technology. Retrieved from https://www.cdt.org/
testimony/cybersecurity-innovative-solutions-challenging-problems
History of the U.S. Bill of Rights. Retrieved from http://www.archives.gov/exhibits/
charters/constitution_history.html
Persuasive Writing: Take a Stand. Retrieved from http://www.pbs.org/now/classroom/
lessonplan-04.html
U.S. Bill of Rights. Retrieved from http://www.archives.gov/exhibits/charters/
bill_of_rights.html

CHAPTER 9: INQUIRY AND CREATIVITY IN ASSESSMENTS

iEARN Collaboration Centre: Connecting Math to Our Lives. Retrieved from http://
media.iearn.org/projects/math
iEARN Collaboration Centre: Mathematics Virtual Learning Circle. Retrieved from
https://media.iearn.org/node/143
Math TV Problem Solving Videos. Retrieved from http://www.mathtv.org/
National Math Trail. Retrieved from http://www.nationalmathtrail.org/
Rubistar. Retrieved from http://rubistar.4teachers.org/
Rubrics for Teachers. Retrieved from http://www.rubrics4teachers.com/
Teachnology: Why Rubrics? Retrieved from http://www.teach-nology.com/tutorials/
teaching/rubrics/
World Climate. Retrieved from http://worldclimate.com
World Factbook. Retrieved from https://www.cia.gov/library/publications/the-world
-factbook/

CHAPTER 10: INQUIRY IN
EDUCATION USING TECHNOLOGY

Epals. Retrieved from http://www.epals.com/
GoogleLitTrips. Retrieved from http://googlelittrips.com

International Society for Educational in Technology (ISTE) Standards for Students. Retrieved from http://www.iste.org/AM/Template.cfm?Section=NETS

Library of Congress: American Memory Project. Retrieved from http://memory.loc .gov

Technology Integration Matrix. Retrieved from http://fcit.usf.edu/matrix/index.html

U.S. Fish and Wildlife Organization: America's National Wildlife Refuge System. Retrieved from http://www.fws.gov/refuges/databases/tes.html

World Wise Schools: Speakers Match. Retrieved from http://wws.peacecorps.gov/wws/

CHAPTER 11: LEARNING AT A DISTANCE

Bloom, B. (1984). *Taxonomy of educational objectives*. Boston, MA: Allyn & Bacon.

Gagne, R. (1995). *The conditions of learning*. New York: Holt, Rinehart & Winston.

Keller, J. (1987). Development and use of the ARCS model of motivational design. *Journal of Instructional Development*, *10*(3), 2–10.

MapQuest. Retrieved from http://www.mapquest.com

National Center for Accessible Media: Tools and Guidelines. Retrieved from http://ncam.wgbh.org/invent_build/web_multimedia/tools-guidelines

About the Author

Dr. Teresa Coffman is nationally recognized for her work in technology integration in K–12 education. A published author on inquiry-oriented learning, Dr. Coffman's focus is on helping teachers use technology to encourage creativity and information literacy for the 21st-century global learner. Currently an associate professor of education at the University of Mary Washington in Fredericksburg, Virginia, she instructs pre-service teachers as they work toward initial licensure and a master's degree in education.